Better Reading

ENGLISH

Better Reading
ENGLISH

Jenni Currie Santamaria

New York   Chicago   San Francisco   Lisbon   London   Madrid   Mexico City
Milan   New Delhi   SanJuan   Singapore   Sydney   Toronto

1 2 3 4 5 6 7 8 9 0   DOC   21 20 19 18 17 16

ISBN: 978-0-07-174476-8
MHID: 0-07-174476-2

e-ISBN: 978-0-07-175192-6
e-MHID: 0-07-175192-0

Special thanks to Hilary Geyer for her assistance in preparing this reader.

Contents

4. The Early United States

5. Entertainment

6. Eating In, Eating Out

7. Playing the Game

8. Sickness and Health

9. Children and Parents

10. Free Time, Fun Time

Preface

Better Reading English has been developed for English speakers who have a basic to intermediate knowledge of English, and is designed to help them read English better and to encourage them to read more.

To read better, we must read more. As an encouragement for beginning readers, I have organized this book according to 10 areas of interest: nature, the 20th century, San Francisco, early U.S. history, entertainment, eating and food choices, popular games, health, family, and leisure time. At least one of these areas should interest the reader immediately, and after that subject is explored, interest in another will follow.

The selections include material that has appeared in magazines and books, as well as on the Internet. Some of the online selections have been abridged and edited for accuracy. Selections not otherwise credited were compiled, adapted, or created by the author. While each section's material relates to a topic in American culture, the section as a whole is not intended to be an overview or summary of the topic. Instead, the selections have been chosen for their broad appeal, their variety, and their likelihood to inspire readers to explore new horizons and to feel confident as they encounter the written word in English in its myriad forms.

Each section begins with the selections that are easiest to read, although none of the material has been simplified. The selections become progressively more difficult within each section. All reading selections are followed by one or more exercises designed to help readers develop skills in understanding what they are reading. The overall goal is to help readers develop reading strategies that will help them understand and benefit from future reading material. If we can read better, we will read more.

How to Use This Book

One of the joys of reading is that you can read what you want, when you want, however you want.

The format of *Better Reading English* enables you to use, and benefit from, the book in different ways. One approach is to select a topic that interests you, read each of the selections in order, writing the exercises after each one, until you have completed the final selection. If you are really interested in this topic, you will probably be able to read the most difficult selections—because you want to and because you have been developing important reading skills that make the material easier to read. Then you may choose another topic that interests you.

A second approach is to read the first, easiest selection in each section, writing the exercises as you go, then progress to the second selection of each section, and so on until you have completed the most difficult selections in the book.

In your approach to an individual selection, first read it in its entirety then proceed with the exercises, which are designed to help you read without the aid of a dictionary. The exercises encourage development of the following skills:

- *Skimming for general meaning*: reading the entire selection quickly to determine its general purpose and content;
- *Scanning for details*: noting headings, references, and other guides to quick information;
- *Using word formation to determine meaning*: knowing how prefixes, suffixes, verb endings, and grammatical forms indicate meaning;
- *Using context to determine meaning*: making educated guesses about the meaning of unfamiliar words by determining their role in the context of a sentence, paragraph, or entire selection;
- *Learning idioms and other expressions*: recognizing and learning the meaning of unusual expressions and phrases;
- *Understanding artistic expression*: recognizing literary devices that authors use;
- *Rereading for comprehension*: reading an entire selection again to gain greater understanding.

Better Reading

ENGLISH

Nature in the United States

YELLOWSTONE PARK RULES

I. PRE-READING

A. Background information

Yellowstone Park is a U.S. national park located mainly in the state of Wyoming. It has mountains, rivers, lakes, hundreds of different kinds of animals, hot-water springs, and an active volcano. More than two million people a year visit Yellowstone Park. In this section, you will read some of the rules for visitors to Yellowstone.

B. Words to know before you read

Match the words to their definitions.

____1. prohibited

____2. allowed

____3. climbing

____4. backcountry

____5. littering

____6. illegal

____7. wildlife

a. throwing trash on the ground or in the water

b. against the law

c. wilderness; area with few people and no buildings

d. wild animals

e. not permitted

f. using hands and feet to go up a mountain

g. permitted

C. Reading strategy

Quickly read the heading for each topic in "Yellowstone Park Rules and Regulations." Then answer the question.

How many topics are there? _____

II. READ

Read the text. Mark the words you don't know, but don't stop reading to look them up.

Yellowstone Park Rules and Regulations

Bicycling

Permitted only on established public roads, parking areas and designated routes, so feel free to bring bikes on your vacation to Yellowstone National Park. However, keep in mind that bicycles are prohibited on boardwalks and backcountry trails.

Boating

This makes for a fun and exciting adventure during your Yellowstone vacation in the park. Be sure to obtain a boating permit before you take to the water. Boaters must have a Coast Guard–approved "wearable" flotation device for each person boating.

Yellowstone Park Boating Permit: A 10-day motorized boat permit costs $10; an annual permit is $20. Non-motorized boat permits cost $5 for 7 days or $10 for the season.

Climbing

A great adventure to include during your Yellowstone vacation. Climbing is allowed in only a few areas of Yellowstone National Park, however it is illegal in the Grand Canyon of the Yellowstone Park area. Contact the backcountry office in Yellowstone for more information.

Disturbing Yellowstone Park features

Possessing, collecting, removing, defacing or destroying any natural or archaeological objects or plants, animals or minerals is prohibited.

Driving

Motorcycles, motor scooters and motorbikes are not allowed off-road or on trails. Operators must have a valid driver's license and vehicles must display valid state license plates.

Seat belts must be worn by all people driving or riding in vehicles. Slow-moving vehicles must pull over to let others pass. Never stop or pause in the middle of the road. Use pullouts! Speed limit is 45 m.p.h.

Feeding wildlife

Is against the law.

Fires

Permitted only in designated Yellowstone camping areas, in picnic areas with fire grates and in some backcountry campsites. Any dead-and-down material may be used as firewood, but chain saws are prohibited. Thoroughly extinguish all fires.

Food

Your food must be attended to while not in storage, and must be stored properly. Never leave food outside your vehicle or in Yellowstone camping areas when you're away or sleeping, as it may very well attract unwelcome visitors.

Littering

Illegal throughout the park and in Yellowstone camping areas.

Pets

Pets are allowed to come with the family on your vacation to Yellowstone National Park; however, certain restrictions (for their own safety) are in place. Whether in a Yellowstone camping area or just exploring the park, pets must be leashed and are prohibited from trails, in the backcountry and in thermal basins. Pets are not allowed more than 100 feet from a road or parking area. Leaving a pet unattended or tied to an object is prohibited.

Source: www.yellowstonepark.com

III. COMPREHENSION CHECK

Mark the sentences T (True) or F (False).

_____ 1. You can bicycle anywhere in Yellowstone Park.

_____ 2. You need a boating permit to use a boat in the park.

_____ 3. Climbing is not permitted in Yellowstone.

_____ 4. You are not allowed to remove plants from the park.

_____ 5. You can drive in the park if you have a license.

_____ 6. It is illegal to feed wildlife in the park.

_____ 7. Fires are not allowed in the park.

_____ 8. You must not leave food on tables while you're away.

_____ 9. Littering is prohibited.

_____ 10. Pets are allowed in the backcountry.

IV. VOCABULARY BUILDING

A. Understanding from context

Read the phrases. Before you look up words in the dictionary, use the context of the sentence to help you match the boldface words and idioms with the definitions below.

_____ 1. **Thoroughly** extinguish all fires.

_____ 2. Be sure to **obtain** a boating permit.

_____ 3. Possessing, collecting, removing, **defacing**, or destroying any natural objects

_____ 4. Fires are permitted only in **designated** Yellowstone camping areas.

_____ 5. Pets are allowed; however, certain **restrictions** are in place.

_____ 6. Leaving a pet **unattended** or tied to an object is prohibited.

_____ 7. Vehicles must **display** valid state license plates.

_____ 8. Vehicles must display **valid** state license plates.

_____ 9. **Feel free** to bring bikes on your vacation.

_____ 10. **Keep in mind** that bicycles are prohibited in some places.
  a. get
  b. alone; with no supervision
  c. to ruin the way something looks, for example, by writing or drawing on it
  d. officially chosen or marked
  e. remember
  f. show
  g. go ahead—there's no problem
  h. limitations; things you can't do
  i. completely
  j. legally acceptable

B. Use the new words

Complete the sentences with the boldface words and idioms from Exercise A.

1. Some kids were _____ the wall by drawing on it.

2. You need to _____ permission to camp here.

3. There are _____ on how many fish you can catch. You can only catch five.

4. His ID card expired last month. It's not _____ anymore.

5. _____ to call me anytime. I'd love to talk to you.

6. You cannot park in spaces _____ for handicapped people.

7. You must _____ your parking permit in the window.

8. Clean your campsite _____. Any food left on the ground will attract animals.

9. _____ that you should wear sunscreen when you go outside.

10. Small children should never be left _____.

C. Classify words

Find these words in the text and decide if they are adjectives or nouns. Write them in the correct place in the chart.

routes

boardwalks

trails

wearable

flotation device

archeological

slow-moving

pullouts

fire grates

chain saws

unwelcome

thermal

adjectives	nouns

D. Identify meaning

Write words from the chart that can replace the underlined words.

Adjectives:

1. Wild animals are <u>not wanted</u> in the campground.

   _____

2. Some scientists use computers that are <u>light enough to wear</u>.

   _____

3. Native Americans have lived in Yellowstone for thousands of years, so there are many <u>ancient historical</u> sites there. _____

4. Large trucks are <u>not fast</u> on mountain roads. _____

5. It's nice to relax in the <u>hot</u> springs. _____

Nouns:

6. They were walking on <u>paths</u> through the forest.

   _____

7. We got lost because we didn't know the <u>way</u>.

   _____

8. He cut down the tree with a <u>mechanical saw</u>.

   _____

9. In Yellowstone, there are <u>wooden walkways</u> over the hot, wet ground.

   _____

10. When you are on a boat, you must wear a <u>life jacket</u>.

    _____

11. The trailer moved to <u>the space on the side of the road</u> so that the cars behind it could go by.

    _____

12. We cooked our meat on the <u>metal frame above the fire</u>.

    _____

V. UNDERSTANDING GRAMMAR: THE PASSIVE VOICE

A. Read about the passive voice

The passive voice is used when the important part of a sentence is the action or the result of the action, not who or what is doing the action. Sometimes the passive voice includes a "by" phrase.

> *Seat belts **must be worn** <u>by all people driving or riding in vehicles</u>.*

Most of the time, the "by" phrase is not included because who or what is doing the action is understood or not important.

> *Pets **must be leashed**.* ("by their owners" is understood)
> *Bicycles **are prohibited**.* ("by park authorities" is understood)

To form the passive voice, the object of the action becomes the subject, and the verb is formed with *be* + past participle. Compare the following active and passive sentences:

Present tense:
    Active: *The park rules **allow** pets.*
    Passive: *Pets **are not allowed** (by the park rules).*

Past tense:
    Active: *The ranger **permitted** us to camp there.*
    Passive: *We **were not permitted** to camp there (by the ranger).*

Modal:
    Active: *You **must store** your food.*
    Passive: *Food **must be stored** (by you).*

B. Identify the passive voice

Read the sentences. Underline the verbs. Label the sentences Active *or* Passive.

1. Congress established Yellowstone National Park in 1872. _____

2. Yellowstone National Park was established in 1872. _____

3. Hundreds of types of animals can be found in the park. _____

4. You can find hundreds of types of animals in the park. _____

5. Tourists may see bears, wolves, bison, and elk in the park. _____

6. Bears, wolves, bison, and elk may be seen in the park. _____

7. You must not take plants or rocks from the park. _____

8. Plants and rocks must not be taken from the park. _____

VI.   READ IT AGAIN

Read the rules again. Answer the questions.

1. Which activities are completely prohibited at Yellowstone Park?

    _____

    _____

    _____

2. Which activities are restricted?

    _____

    _____

    _____

GRAND CANYON NATIONAL PARK

I. PRE-READING

A. Background information

The Grand Canyon is one of the most famous U.S. national parks. It is located in northern Arizona. It is 277 miles long, from 4 to 18 miles wide, and in some places 1 mile deep.

B. Words to know before you read

Match the words to their definitions.

_____ 1.	lodging	a.	edge
_____ 2.	congestion	b.	difficult, requiring exertion
_____ 3.	facilities	c.	can be reached or entered
_____ 4.	accessible	d.	a place to stay temporarily
_____ 5.	rim	e.	space or equipment for doing something
_____ 6.	elevation	f.	when something is blocked or full of traffic
_____ 7.	strenuous	g.	height above sea level

C. Reading strategy

Scan the following text as quickly as you can. Look for the answer to this question.

How far above sea level is the North Rim? _____

II. READ

Read the text. Mark the words you don't know, but don't stop reading to look them up.

Grand Canyon National Park Service

Grand Canyon National Park receives an average of 5 million visitors a year; this means the park is crowded most of the year. Expect heavy crowds during spring, summer, and fall months. During these months reservations for camping and lodging are essential for overnight visitors. Day-use visitors should expect traffic congestion and parking problems, particularly in summer. The least crowded time is November through February. However, winter weather is a major consideration when planning a trip during these months.

Most visitors come to the South Rim (open all year). The North Rim (open mid-May through mid-October only) has fewer facilities and is less accessible (it is over 200 miles one way by automobile from the South Rim to the North Rim, a 5-hour drive for most). When making reservations for lodging and camping, remember to identify the rim you plan on visiting.

The South Rim of Grand Canyon averages 7,000 feet above sea level, the North Rim over 8,000 feet above sea level. Visitors with respiratory or heart problems may experience difficulties; all walking at this elevation can be strenuous.

Source: www.usparkinfo.com/grandcanyon.html

III. COMPREHENSION CHECK

Write answers to the questions.

1. How many visitors does the Grand Canyon get every year?

   _____

2. Which seasons are crowded?

   _____

3. What do you have to consider if you want to visit in winter?

   _____

4. Which rim do most people visit?

   _____

5. When is the North Rim open?

   _____

6. How long does it take to drive from the South Rim to the North Rim?

   _____

7. Why might visitors with heart problems have difficulty at the Grand Canyon?

   _____

IV. VOCABULARY BUILDING

<u>A.</u> Word families

Read the word families in the chart. Then choose the correct form for each sentence.

noun	Verb	Adjective
1. crowd		crowded
2. reservation	reserve	reserved
3. congestion		congested
4. consideration	consider	considerate
5. access	access	accessible
6. identification	identify	identifiable
7. difficulty		difficult

1. a. We couldn't find parking because the lot was so _____.

   b. There was a large _____ of people looking at the canyon.

2. a. You need to _____ a room if you want to spend the night.

   b. We don't have a _____ for Friday night, but we have a place to stay Saturday night.

   c. I'm sorry, you can't sit there. That table is _____.

3. a. They set a limit on the number of visitors because the park roads were getting _____.

   b. The _____ downtown is terrible. We need better public transportation.

4. a. You need to _____ the weather before you travel in the winter.

   b. He always thinks of others. He is kind and _____.

   c. One important _____ is whether to camp or stay in a cabin.

5. a. Sometimes there is no _____ to the North Rim because of the snow.

   b. The South Rim is always _____ because it is at a lower elevation.

   c. I couldn't _____ the reservation site because Internet service wasn't working.

6. a. A park ranger can _____ plants and animals for you.

   b. I saw an animal in the forest, but it was too far away to be _____.

   c. You'll need to show _____ when you get on the airplane.

7. a. If you have heart problems, you may have _____ walking at the Grand Canyon.

   b. It is _____ to describe how beautiful the canyon is.

V. UNDERSTANDING GRAMMAR: *FEWER* AND *LESS*

A. Read about comparisons with *fewer* and *less*

Fewer is used for comparisons. It means *a smaller number*, and it's only used with plural nouns.

> The North Rim has **fewer** facilities than the South Rim.
> The North Rim gets **fewer** visitors than the South Rim.
> The Grand Canyon has **fewer** large animals than Yellowstone.

Less is usually used with adjectives and non-count nouns.

> The North Rim is **less** accessible than the South Rim.
> The South Rim gets **less** snow than the North Rim.
> The North Rim is **less** crowded than the South Rim.

B. Use the grammar.

Fill in the blanks with less *or* fewer.

Are you trying to decide whether to spend your vacation at the Grand Canyon or at Yellowstone? They are both very beautiful, but here are a few things to consider: If you have a short vacation, you may want to choose the Grand Canyon because it takes 1) _____ time to visit (unless you are going to hike to the bottom of the canyon). If you have a longer vacation, you may want to try Yellowstone because there are 2) _____ things to do at the Grand Canyon. At Yellowstone you can climb, go boating, visit hot springs, and see large animals. There are bison, bears, wolves, and elk at Yellowstone. There are 3) _____ large animals to see at the Grand Canyon.
    You should also think about the time of year. In the summer it may be hotter at the Grand Canyon. In the winter Yellowstone may be 4) _____ accessible. Yellowstone gets 5) _____ visitors in the off-season, so if you don't like crowds, you may want to go there.

VI. READ IT AGAIN

Answer the questions.

1. Why is it necessary to reserve lodgings before you go to the Grand Canyon?

    _____

    _____

2. What are the advantages and disadvantages of going to the North Rim?

    _____

    _____

SAVING TREES

I. PRE-READING

A. Background information

John Muir was a naturalist (someone who studies nature) and a writer who lived from 1838 to 1914. He wrote many books and articles about his adventures in nature. Muir fought hard to preserve forests and mountains, especially Yosemite Valley and Sequoia National Park in California. The reading for this section is part of a letter he wrote about saving the Sequoia trees.
    Sequoias (also called redwoods) are very large, very old trees that grow in the Sierra Nevada Mountains in California. The wood from Sequoias isn't good for building—it breaks easily—but many of the trees were cut down in the late 1800s anyway. Because of the work of John Muir and others, these trees are now protected and can be enjoyed by visitors today.

B. Words to know before you read

Match the words to their definitions.

___ 1.	fool	a.	large; having great power
___ 2.	aboriginal	b.	having many things happening
___ 3.	mighty	c.	a long time with not enough water
___ 4.	eventful	d.	a factory where trees are sawed into wood
___ 5.	drought	e.	original inhabitant; native
___ 6.	sawmills	f.	a person who is silly or stupid

C. Reading strategy

Quickly read the following paragraph. Then answer the question.

How old are the oldest Sequoia trees? _____

II. READ

Read the paragraph. Mark the words you don't know, but don't stop reading to look them up.

Any fool can destroy trees. They cannot defend themselves or run away. And few destroyers of trees ever plant any; nor can planting avail much toward restoring our grand aboriginal giants. It took more than three thousand years to make some of the oldest of the Sequoias, trees that are still standing in perfect strength and beauty, waving and singing in the mighty forests of the Sierra. Through all the eventful centuries since Christ's time, and long before that, God has cared for these trees, saved them from drought, disease, avalanches, and a thousand storms; but he cannot save them from sawmills and fools; this is left to the American people.

Source: "Save the Redwoods," John Muir. *Sierra Club Bulletin*, Volume XI, Number 1: January 1920, pp. 1–4, http://www.yosemite.ca.us/john_muir_writings

III. COMPREHENSION CHECK

Circle the letter of the sentences with the same meaning.

1. *Any fool can destroy trees. They cannot defend themselves or run away.*

   a. It's easy to destroy trees because they can't protect themselves.

   b. Only stupid people destroy trees.

2. *. . .nor can planting avail much toward restoring our grand aboriginal giants. It took more than three thousand years to make some of the oldest Sequoias.*

   a. People who destroy trees should plant new ones.

   b. Planting new trees doesn't help because the Sequoias are so old.

3. . . . .*trees that are still standing in perfect strength and beauty, waving and singing in the mighty forests of the Sierra.*

   a. The trees can move their arms and sing.

   b. The trees move and make pleasing sounds in the wind.

4. *Through all the eventful centuries since Christ's time, and long before that, God has cared for these trees,*

   a. The trees have lived for hundreds of years.

   b. The trees have always had protection.

5. . . .*but he cannot save them from sawmills and fools; this is left to the American people.*

   a. No one can save the trees from the people who want to cut them down.

   b. The American people need to save the trees.

IV. VOCABULARY BUILDING

A. Natural disasters and other problems

Read the following natural disaster words and their definitions.

drought	*a long period with not enough water*
disease	*illness; sickness*
avalanche	*a large amount of snow, ice, and rocks falling down a mountainside*
blizzard	*a heavy snowstorm*
mudslide	*a large amount of mud (wet dirt) sliding down a mountain*
flood	*a large amount of water in an area that should be dry*

B. Identify the problem

Write the correct word from Exercise A next to each description.

1. He walked slowly toward the house, which he could barely see through the swirling snow. _____

2. The earth got hard, the plants dried up, the lakes disappeared, and the landscape turned yellow and brown. _____

3. They spent the whole day piling up sandbags to protect their home from the rising river, but in the end the water filled the lower level of the house. _____

4. She lay in the hospital bed, thin and pale except for the red blotches covering most of her body. _____

5. The skiers heard the distant rumble of the mountainside crashing down and felt immense relief that they were so far away.

   _____

6. After a month of rain, the hillside gave way, filling the yards and in some cases the living rooms of the houses below with brown mud.

   _____

V. UNDERSTANDING GRAMMAR: *IT + TAKES*

A. Read about expressing length of time with *it + takes*

We express length of time using *it + takes* + an infinitive verb.

> *It **took** more than three thousand years for the oldest Sequoias **to grow**.*

In the present tense:

> South Rim to North Rim of the Grand Canyon—5.5-hour drive

> *It **takes** five and a half hours **to drive** from the South Rim to the North Rim of the Grand Canyon.*

We can express the same idea two ways in the past tense.

> The loggers cut down the giant tree in three hours.
> *It **took** the loggers three hours **to cut down** the giant tree.*

B. Use the grammar

Read the tour guide facts, and write sentences to express the lengths of time.

1. Las Vegas to the Grand Canyon—five-hour drive

   _____

2. South Rim to North Rim—25-mile hike

   _____

3. Through the Grand Canyon on the Colorado River—17-day raft

   _____

4. Muir and others stopped the logging in Sequoia, a national park—nine years

   _____

5. Reinhold Metzger backpacked the 211-mile John Muir trail—six days

   _____

VI. READ IT AGAIN

Answer the questions.

1. Muir uses the word *fool* twice. Who is he talking about?

   _____

2. Muir uses poetic language to talk about the trees: *grand aboriginal giants...standing in perfect strength and beauty, waving and singing in the mighty forests*...Why does he use this kind of language to describe the trees?

_____

AN OUTDOOR SURVIVAL SCHOOL

I. PRE-READING

A. Background information

This excerpt is from an article in the *New York Times* about a class at an "outdoor survival school." People take the class to learn how to survive if something goes wrong when they are camping or hiking. They spend two days in the wilderness with only a knife, a parachute cord, a fire sparker, and a water bottle. They are not allowed to bring a tent or anything to sleep on. Mr. Posner is one of the students in the class. Mr. Nestor is the teacher.

B. Words to know before you read

Match the words to their definitions.

_____1. acorn

_____2. devour

_____3. laboring

_____4. pine needles

_____5. insulation

_____6. broth

a. eat hungrily

b. a covering to keep something or someone warm

c. a small nut that is the fruit of the oak tree

d. working

e. thin soup

f. the thin needlelike leaves of a pine tree

C. Reading strategy

Quickly scan the following paragraphs for names and numbers. Then answer the questions.

1. How does Mr. Posner feel? _____

2. What was the temperature at night? _____

Setting Out into the Arizona Wilderness with only a Knife

The group, ravenous with hunger, began the laborious process of shelling acorns, which were dropped into a rusty can we had found. Then we boiled up an acorn-and-wild-onion broth and devoured it ravenously. But we were all still hungry. Despite laboring for much of the day collecting onions and acorns we still couldn't fill our bellies.

"I'm so hungry I could eat a squirrel," Mr. Posner said morosely. Mr. Nestor explained that in an emergency situation hunting could burn up more calories, especially when there was a chance of not actually catching anything.

The long night stretched out ahead of us. The temperature dropped to 36 degrees. The soaring darkness of the woods enclosed as the needling cold stabbed into our clothing. We lay on our beds of prickly pine needles, sticking some into our clothes for extra insulation. We fed the fire to stay warm. The smoke from the fire pit billowed into our eyes, turning them bloodshot and sooty. We either roasted in the shelter or froze when we fell asleep and the fire died.

A gray dawn woke us early. Despite lack of sleep and a gnawing hunger with little food for 24 hours, there was a sense of pride we had survived the night.

Source: "Setting Out into the Arizona Wilderness with only a Knife," Jonathan Green, *New York Times*, November 10, 2006, http://travel.nytimes.com

II. COMPREHENSION CHECK

Mark the sentences T (True) or F (False).

_____ 1.   They ate acorn and wild onion soup.

_____ 2.   It didn't take long to collect the onions and acorns.

_____ 3.   They were full after they ate the broth.

_____ 4.   Mr. Posner was very hungry.

_____ 5.   Mr. Nestor said that they shouldn't hunt because they would burn more calories.

_____ 6.   They slept on pine needles.

_____ 7.   They used pine needles to help keep them warm.

_____ 8.   The fire was very smoky.

_____ 9.   They were still warm when the fire went out.

_____ 10. In the morning they were proud of themselves.

III. VOCABULARY BUILDING

A. Adjectives

This article contains many descriptive adjectives. Read the following definitions and sentences. Then choose the correct adjective for each sentence below.

ravenous   *very hungry*

  We hadn't eaten all day, and we were ravenous.

laborious   *requiring a lot work; filled with labor*

  After a long, laborious day, we finished building the shelter.

rusty   *covered with a reddish-brown color, as in oxidized metal*

  The knife that fell in the water got rusty.

soaring   *to be very high or tall*

>   The soaring bird was hit by an airplane.

prickly   *having sharp points*

>   The prickly plants made small cuts in his hands.

bloodshot   *having red lines in the white part of the eye*

>   He slept very little and woke up with bloodshot eyes.

sooty   *covered with the black powder from something burning*

>   After cleaning the fireplace, the boy's clothes were sooty.

1.   The dry grass was _____ and uncomfortable.

2.   The old car was damaged and _____.

3.   After the fire, everything in the house was black and _____.

4.   The _____ dogs ate everything they could find.

5.   She spent many _____ hours finishing the project.

6.   The smoke from the campfire gave them _____ eyes.

7.   The _____ clouds were almost black; we knew a storm was coming.

B. Verbs

In addition to adjectives, the article uses many verbs. Read the following definitions and sentences. Then choose the correct verb for each sentence below. These are verbs—you may need to change the form to fit the sentence.

shell   *to remove the shell of a nut or pea*

>   It's easy to shell a walnut if you have the right tool.

boil   *to cook in hot, bubbling water*

>   She prefers to boil eggs because they are less fattening that way.

collect   *to bring things together*

>   They collected wood to make a fire.

stick (past tense: *stuck*)   *to push a pointed object into something*

>   She stuck the needle in the cushion so she wouldn't lose it.

enclose   *to surround; to close off on all sides*

>   He enclosed the rabbits in a cage so they wouldn't run away.

feed (past tense: *fed*)   *to give food*

>   It's illegal to feed the animals in a national park.

billow (when used with steam, clouds, or smoke)   *to move out in a wavelike motion*

> The dark clouds billowed across the sky.

roast   *to cook in the oven; to become very hot*

> While the turkey was roasting in the oven, I felt like I was roasting in the kitchen.

freeze (past tense: *froze*)   *to turn into ice; to become very cold*

> My mother always thinks I'll freeze if I don't wear a jacket.

1. They threw bread in the lake to _____ the ducks.

2. The smoke _____ out of the chimney.

3. She felt like she was going to _____ in the hot sun.

4. We _____ ourselves in a shelter to protect us from the animals.

5. They had to _____ the peas before they cooked them.

6. He _____ his knife into the tree.

7. They _____ in the snow after the avalanche took their shelter.

8. We _____ water over the fire to cook our pasta.

9. He _____ beautiful rocks of many shapes and colors.

IV.   UNDERSTANDING GRAMMAR: DESPITE

A.   Read about *despite*

Despite is a preposition used to show an opposition, or an unexpected result.

> **Despite** *laboring for much of the day collecting onions and acorns, we still couldn't fill our bellies.*
> **Despite** *lack of sleep and a gnawing hunger with little food for 24 hours, there was a sense of pride we had survived the night.*

Despite has the same meaning as *even though*, but it is followed by a gerund or a noun, not by a clause. Compare these sentences:

> *Even though **it was cold**, we didn't make a fire.*
> *Despite **the cold**, we didn't make a fire.*

> *Even though **it was crowded**, I enjoyed the Grand Canyon.*
> *Despite **the crowds**, I enjoyed the Grand Canyon.*

B. Use the grammar

Rewrite the sentences with despite.

1. **Even though** *it was raining*, **we went for a hike.**

   _____

2. **Even though** *it was difficult*, **we finished the project.**

   _____

3. **Even though** *it was congested*, **the city was beautiful.**

   _____

V. READ IT AGAIN

Answer the questions.

1. How did the wilderness class spend their day?

   _____

2. How did they keep warm at night?

   _____

EXCERPT FROM *HATCHET* BY GARY PAULSEN

I. PRE-READING

A. Background information

Hatchet is a very famous novel by Gary Paulsen about a boy named Brian. While he is traveling on a small plane to visit his father, the pilot has a heart attack and dies. Brian has to land the plane in the forest. It crashes into a lake, and Brian has nothing to help him survive except a hatchet. (A hatchet is a small axe.) Brian faces many dangers in the forest, including hunger, a tornado, and animal attacks, but he learns how to survive.

B. Words to know before you read

Match the words to their definitions.

1. detach		a. a large deer with horns
2. fur		b. hard pointed things growing out of animal's head
3. horns		c. dirt or mud
4. lungs		d. the organs used for breathing
5. moose		e. to separate from the surroundings
6. muck		f. animal hair

<u>C.</u> Reading strategy

Quickly read the selection. Then answer the question.

What did the moose do to Brian? _____

II. READ

Read the text. Mark the words you don't know, but don't stop reading to look them up.

It was very nearly the last act of his life. Later he would not know why he started to turn—some smell or sound. A tiny brushing sound. But something caught his ear or nose and he began to turn, and had his head half around, when he a saw a brown wall of fur detach itself from the forest to his rear and come down on him like a runaway truck. He just had time to see that it was a moose—he knew them from pictures but did not know, could not guess how large they were—when it hit him. It was a cow and she had horns, but she took him in the left side of the back with her forehead, took him and threw him out into the water and then came after him to finish the job.

He had another half second to fill his lungs with air and she was on him again, using her head to drive him down into the mud of the bottom. *Insane*, he thought. Just that, the word *insane*. Mud filled his eyes, his ears, the horn boss on the moose drove him deeper and deeper into the bottom muck, and suddenly it was over and he felt alone.

Source: *Hatchet*, by Gary Paulson, New York: Simon & Schuster, 1987

III. COMPREHENSION CHECK

Circle the letter of the sentence or phrase with the same meaning.

1. *. . .but something caught his ear or nose. . .*

    a. Something touched his ear or nose.

    b. He heard or smelled something.

2. *. . .he a saw a brown wall of fur detach itself from the forest. . .*

    a. There was a lot of animal hair in the forest.

    b. He suddenly saw a large brown animal.

3. *. . .come down on him like a runaway truck.*

    a. come very fast

    b. run over him

4. *It was a cow and she had horns. . .*

    a. It wasn't a moose.

    b. It was a female.

5. . . .*and then came after him to finish the job.*

    a. came after him to kill him

    b. came after him because she had work to do

6. . . .*using her head to drive him down into the mud. . .*

    a. pushing him into the mud

    b. pulling him into the mud

IV. VOCABULARY BUILDING

A. Words to describe animals

Look up the words to describe animals. Then write the words in the chart under the correct animal. A word may be repeated.

horns

fur

paws

claws

beak

gills

scales

tail

whiskers

fin

hooves

feather

tiger	salmon	hawk	bison

B. Use the vocabulary

Write the correct animal name from the table in each sentence.

1. The _____ padded through the long grass on giant paws, the stripes on its fur making it hard to distinguish from the plants behind it.

2. Spying its prey far below, the _____ descended, claws outstretched and beak ready to snap up the unsuspecting creature.

3. They heard the hooves of the _____ thundering through the field.

4. The _____ flopped on the deck, gills gasping for air and scales glistening in the sun.

V. UNDERSTANDING GRAMMAR: REPEATED COMPARATIVES

__A.__ Read about comparatives

Review these rules for comparative adjectives:

For most comparatives with one-syllable adjectives, add -er.

> warm—warm*er*

Comparatives for words ending in -y add -ier.

> healthy—health*ier*

Comparatives for other words with two or more syllables use "more."

> *more* interesting

These comparatives are irregular:

> good—better
>
> bad—worse
>
> far—farther (or further)
>
> fun—more fun

__B.__ Use repeated comparatives

A repeated comparative gives the idea that something is increasing in strength, quality, or quantity.

> *The moose drove him **deeper and deeper** into the bottom muck.*
> *He ran **faster and faster**.*
> *He got **more and more tired**.*

Complete the sentences with a repeated comparative. Use these adjectives:

hungry

dark

frustrated

thin

easy

1. The night sky grew

   _____.

2. As the days went by and he couldn't find food, he got

   _____.

3. As he learned more, surviving in the forest slowly got

   _____.

4. He tried and tried to catch fish but couldn't, and this made him

   _____.

5. He noticed that his body was changing, that he was getting

   _____.

VI. READ IT AGAIN

Answer the questions.

1. How did Brian first notice the moose?

   _____

2. Why didn't Brian die in the moose attack?

   _____

The 20th Century

TECHNOLOGY TIME LINE

I. PRE-READING

A. Background information

Technology has changed so much over the last 100 years that it can be surprising to look at a time line showing what happened when. This time line from the PBS show *The American Experience* reminds us of some of the important events that took place in the 1960s–1980s, at the beginning of the computer age.

B. Words to know before you read

Match the words to their definitions.

_____ 1. fiber   a. a small device that is the "brain" of a computer

_____ 2. scanner   b. legal ownership of an idea or design

_____ 3. microprocessor   c. not real; fabricated

_____ 4. launch   d. a long, thin strand

_____ 5. artificial   e. a machine for reading bar codes

_____ 6. patent   f. send into orbit

C. Reading strategy

Read the sentences. Place a check mark by the events that you think happened in the 1980s. Then quickly read the heading for each topic in the time line and check your answers.

_____ People started playing video games.

_____ Stores began using bar codes on items for sale.

_____ The first space shuttle went up.

_____ PCs became popular.

II. READ

Read the text. Mark the words you don't know, but don't stop reading to look them up.

1969 Moon Landing
Millions watch worldwide as the landing module of NASA's Apollo 11 spacecraft touches down on the moon's surface and Neil Armstrong becomes the first human to set foot on the moon. President John F. Kennedy, who vowed to the world that the United States would put a human on the moon before 1970, has not lived to witness the moment.

1970 Optical Fiber
Corning Glass announces it has created a glass fiber so clear that it can communicate pulses of light. GTE and AT&T will soon begin experiments to transmit sound and image data using fiber optics, which will transform the communications industry.

1972 Video Game
Pong, one of the first mass-produced video games, has become the rage.

1974 Bar code
The first shipments of bar-coded products arrive in American stores. Scanners at checkout stations read the codes using laser technology.

1975 Microsoft
Old high school friends Bill Gates and Paul Allen form a partnership known as Microsoft to write computer software. They sell their first software to Ed Roberts at MIT, which has produced the Altair 8800, the first microprocessor-based computer. Gates soon drops out of Harvard.

1981 Space Shuttle
For the first time, NASA successfully launches and lands its reusable spacecraft, the space shuttle. The shuttle can be used to launch, retrieve, and repair satellites and can serve as a laboratory for physical experiments. While extremely successful, the shuttle program will suffer a disaster in 1986 when the shuttle *Challenger* explodes after takeoff, killing all on board.

1982 Artificial Heart
Dr. Robert Jarvik implants a permanent artificial heart, the Jarvik 7, into Dr. Barney Clark. The heart, powered by an external compressor, keeps Clark alive for 112 days.

1983 PC
In January *Time* names its 1982 "man" of the year—the personal computer. PCs have taken the world by storm, dramatically changing the way people

communicate. IBM dominates the personal computer market, benefiting both from the production of its own machines as well as "clones" produced by other companies.

1985 Genetic Engineering

The USDA [United States Department of Agriculture] gives the go-ahead for the sale of the first genetically altered organism. The rapidly growing biotech industry will seek numerous patents, including one for a tomato that can be shipped when ripe.

Source: "The American Experience Technology Timeline," pbs.org

III. COMPREHENSION CHECK

Mark the sentences T (True) or F (False).

_____ 1. President Kennedy saw Neil Armstrong walk on the moon.

_____ 2. Optical fiber was used to send pictures.

_____ 3. Pong was a popular video game.

_____ 4. Bill Gates created the first microprocessor-based computer.

_____ 5. The space shuttle was used to repair satellites.

_____ 6. In 1983, the most popular PCs were made by IBM.

IV. VOCABULARY BUILDING

A. Understanding from context

Read the sentences. Use the context of the sentence to help you match the boldface expressions and idioms with the definitions below.

_____ 1. Many people watched when the space shuttle **touched down** in Florida for the last time in 2011.

_____ 2. No human has ever **set foot on** Mars.

_____ 3. For most people, **dropping out of** school is not a good idea.

_____ 4. Sometimes a musical group **takes the world by storm** and then disappears a few years later.

_____ 5. The military couldn't act until the President **gave the go-ahead**.
  a. to quit
  b. to walk somewhere or go somewhere
  c. to give permission
  d. to land
  e. to become very popular very quickly

B. Identify meaning

Find the words from Exercise A in the time line. Then answer the questions.

1. What **land**ed on the moon in 1969?

_____

2. Who was the first person **to walk** on the moon?

_____

3. Who **quit** college to start a business?

_____

4. What had **become very popular** by 1983?

_____

5. What did the USDA **give permission** for?

_____

C. Identify meaning

Find and underline these verbs in the time line. Then rewrite the following sentences using the verbs in place of the underlined words. Use the correct verb form.

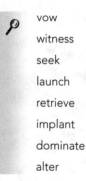

vow

witness

seek

launch

retrieve

implant

dominate

alter

1. The old man had <u>seen</u> many historic events.

_____

2. NASA <u>sends</u> spaceships <u>into orbit</u> from Cape Canaveral, Florida.

_____

3. The shuttle was able to <u>bring back</u> satellites that no longer worked.

_____

4. They use genetic engineering to <u>change</u> plants and animals.

_____

5. The president <u>promised</u> to do many things.

_____

6. It's dangerous for one company to <u>control</u> the market.

_____

7. Scientists are always <u>looking for</u> ways to increase the food supply.

_____

8. They say that someday we will <u>put</u> communication devices <u>under our skin</u>.

_____

V. UNDERSTANDING GRAMMAR: NARRATIVE PRESENT

A. Read about the narrative present

Although all of the events in this time line occurred in the past, you will notice that the verbs are in the present tense. When writers tell a story in the present tense, it's called the narrative present. It's used to make events sound more immediate—as if they are happening now—and can make a story sound more interesting. People often use the narrative present in speaking, and it's often used in journalistic writing.

Look at the charts to review the form of present tense statements.

affirmative	
I You We They	see.
He She It	see**s**.

negative		
I You We They	don't	see.
He She It	doesn't	see.

B. Use the narrative present

Rewrite the sentences using the narrative present.

1. 1990

   Tim Berners-Lee created the World Wide Web.

   _____

2. 1995

   The DVD was invented.

   _____

3. 2001

   Apple Computer announced the release of the iPod.

   _____

4. 2003

    Toyota produced its first hybrid car.

    _____

5. 2005

    Time magazine named YouTube the invention of the year.

    _____

6. 2008

    For the first time, people in the United States sent more text messages than they made phone calls.

    _____

7. 2009

    Movies in 3-D became the rage.

    _____

8. 2010

    The Apple iPad came out and sold millions of units.

VI. READ IT AGAIN

Read the time line in Part II again. Answer the question.

Which of the inventions mentioned in the time line has medical implications?

_____

BILL GATES AT COLLEGE

I. PRE-READING

A. Background information

Everyone knows who Bill Gates is—one of the richest men in the world, the founder of Microsoft, and the creator, with his wife, of the Bill and Melinda Gates Foundation, which gives millions of dollars every year to help people in need. These paragraphs from a biography of Bill Gates tell about the impression he made on a classmate when he was in college. It also describes the moment in 1975 that led to him and his friend Paul Allen selling their first software.

B. Words to know before you read

poker	*a card game that people play for money*
Aiken Computer Center	*a computer center at Harvard University*
Currier House	*a residence at Harvard*

kiosk	*a small structure for selling things, often newspapers and magazines*
toggle switches	*switches for turning things off and on*
BASIC	*a computer programming language first created in the 1960s*

C. Reading strategy

Scan the text as quickly as you can. Look for the answer to this question.

What did Paul Allen see on the cover of a magazine?

II. READ

Read the text. Mark the words you don't know, but don't stop reading to look them up.

When Gates wasn't playing poker at night, he was usually working in the Aiken Computer Center. That was when the machines were least used. Sometimes, an exhausted Gates would fall asleep on computer worktables instead of returning to his room at Currier House. "There were many mornings when I would find him dead asleep on the tables," recalled Leitner, a graduate math student who was also interested in computers. "I remember thinking he was not going to amount to anything. He seemed like a hacker, a nerd. I knew he was bright, but with those glasses, his dandruff, sleeping on tables, you sort of formed that impression. I obviously didn't see the future as clearly as he did."

But Paul Allen saw the future. He may have seen it even more clearly than Gates.

On a cold winter day in December 1974, Allen was walking across Harvard Square in Cambridge on his way to visit Gates, when he stopped at a kiosk and spotted the upcoming January issue of *Popular Electronics*, a magazine he had read regularly since childhood. This issue, however, sent his heart pounding. On the cover was a picture of the Altair 8080, a rectangular metal machine with toggle switches and lights on the front. "World's First Microcomputer Kit to Rival Commercial Models," screamed the magazine cover headline.

"I bought a copy, read it, and raced back to Bill's dorm to talk to him," said Allen, who was still working at Honeywell in nearby Boston. "I told Bill, 'Well, here's our opportunity to do something with BASIC.'"

Gates knew Allen was right. It was time. The personal computer miracle was going to happen.

Source: *Hard Drive: Bill Gates and the Making of the Microsoft Empire*, by James Wallace and Jim Erickson, New York: HarperCollins, 1992, pp. 66–67

III. COMPREHENSION CHECK

Mark the sentences T (True) or F (False).

_____ 1. Gates spent many hours at the computer.

_____ 2. Leitner thought Gates would be very successful.

_____ 3. Paul Allen saw a computer on the cover of *Popular Electronics*.

_____ 4. Allen had never read *Popular Electronics* before.

_____ 5. Allen told Gates about the Altair 8080.

IV. VOCABULARY BUILDING

Read the definitions. Then use the words and expressions to complete the following sentences. Use the correct verb form, and make nouns plural if necessary.

instead of	in place of
give the impression	give an idea or feeling
not amount to anything	not be successful
hacker	a skillful computer programmer; sometimes one who uses computers illegally. (In the paragraph, Leitner uses the word negatively to mean someone who is clever with computers but isn't serious or respectable.)
nerd	a person without social skills; usually refers to someone interested in science, technology, or academic subjects
bright	intelligent
dandruff	small pieces of dead skin in the hair
to spot	to notice
to rival	to give competition to; to be as good as
race	run; try to beat an opponent
dorm	short for "dormitory," a student residence

1. He _____ that he was just a nerd, but he was much more than that.

2. You have to be careful with your passwords to protect yourself from _____.

3. Technology companies _____ to invent new devices and software.

4. University students usually live in the _____ for the first year or two of school.

5. They called him a _____ because he was more interested in computers than in socializing.

6. Gates started a company _____ staying in college.

7. Only very _____ students are admitted to Harvard.

8. His _____ left white specks on his shoulders.

9. Nowadays Apple and Google _____ Microsoft in the technology market.

10. When Allen _____ the Altair 8080 on the magazine cover, he saw the opportunity right away.

11. His classmate thought that he would _____ _____, but he became one of the most successful people in the world.

V. UNDERSTANDING GRAMMAR: PAST CONTINUOUS

A. Read about the past continuous

The past continuous shows an ongoing action in the past. It is often used to show actions that are happening at the same time.

> When he **wasn't playing** poker, he **was working** in the computer lab.

It's also used to show an ongoing action that was interrupted by another action.

> He **was walking** across Harvard Square **when he spotted** the magazine cover.

Sometimes it is used to show that something is taking place at the same time as the rest of the action in the story.

> Allen **was** still **working** at Honeywell (as the events of the story were happening).

Look at the charts to review the form of past continuous statements:

affirmative		
I He She It	was	walk**ing**.
You We They	were	

negative		
I He She It	wasn't	walk**ing**.
You We They	weren't	

B. Use the past continuous

Complete the sentences with the past continuous. Use the verbs in parentheses.

1. Gates _____ at Harvard University when he started the company that would become Microsoft. (study)

2. Allen and Gates met while they _____ high school. (attend)

3. Other programmers _____ to make a deal with Altair, but Gates and Allen were successful. (try)

4. When Paul Allen left Microsoft in 1983, it _____ one of the world's biggest companies. (become)

VI. READ IT AGAIN

Read the paragraphs about Bill Gates again. Answer the question.

Why was Paul Allen's heart pounding when he saw the Altair 8080?

_____

_____

_____

_____

_____

ROCK AGAINST THE BERLIN WALL

I. PRE-READING

A. Background information

The Berlin Wall separated East and West Germany from 1961 to 1989. It was a symbol of the separation between the Communist countries and the Western democracies. Most people would say the Wall came down for economic reasons or because of the policies of Russian president Mikhail Gorbachev and U.S. president Ronald Reagan. But the writer of this article points out that rock 'n' roll music played a part in bringing down the Wall.

B. Words to know before you read

precipitate	*cause*
downfall	*defeat; ruin*
enslaved	*not free*
disturbance	*trouble; interference*
amplifier	*a device to make sounds louder, usually used with music*

loudspeaker   *a device that converts electronic signals to sound; may be used with an amplifier*

clubbed   *hit with a stick*

C. Reading strategy

Scan the text as quickly as you can. Look for the answer to this question.

What British rock groups played at the Berlin Wall concert in 1987?

_____

II. READ

Read the text. Mark the words you don't know, but don't stop reading to look them up.

Rock Helped Roll Away Berlin Wall

As it turns out, President John Kennedy didn't precipitate the downfall of old-style Communism when he stood outside the Berlin City Hall 26 years ago and said "when one man is enslaved, all are not free."

If there was one precipitating event, it was probably the East German disturbances set off by a rock 'n' roll concert two summers ago.

Three British rock groups—David Bowie, the Eurythmics, and Genesis—set up their amplifiers at the Brandenburg Gate on June 6–8, 1987.

For three nights their loudspeakers blasted hard-rock sounds across the Wall. Thousands of young East Berliners clustered on their side, hoping to attend the concert.

When the police and security agents tried to chase them away, the crowd started chanting, "The Wall must go" and "Gorbachev, Gorbachev."

After years of silence, this was the first of the East German protests of the 1980s—the one that everyone below the age of 30 remembers.

The state-controlled East German media didn't let on that there had been a demonstration, even though at least 50 people were arrested and many were clubbed.

Source: "Rock Helped Roll Away Berlin Wall," by Joseph Albright, *Lawrence Daily Journal-World*, November 19, 1989, Cox News Service

III. COMPREHENSION CHECK

Write answers to the questions.

1. Where was Kennedy when he said that if one person isn't free, then no one is free?

_____

2. What time of year was the rock concert?

_____

3. How long was the concert?

   _____

4. What did the police try to do?

   _____

5. Who remembers this protest?

   _____

IV. VOCABULARY BUILDING

A. Verbs and nouns

These words can be used as verbs or nouns. Choose one word for each pair of sentences, using the correct verb form and making nouns plural if necessary.

chase

blast

cluster

chant

arrest

1. **a.** The police _____ the demonstrator down the street.

   b. He ran fast, so the _____ lasted a long time.

2. **a.** They heard a loud _____ from the explosion.

   b. The neighbors complained because he was _____ his music.

3. **a.** The people _____ around the wall trying to hear the music.

   b. There was a large _____ of people near the gate.

4. **a.** The crowd sang several different _____.

   b. They _____ very loudly.

5. **a.** The police made many _____ at the demonstration.

   b. The police _____ the demonstrators.

B. Phrasal verbs

Read the definitions. Then complete the following sentences with the phrasal verbs.

set off   *cause to occur or explode*

*The disturbances were **set off** by a rock concert.*

let on   *admit*

*The government didn't **let on** that there had been a demonstration.*

turn out   result

It **turned out** that Kennedy didn't cause the fall of the Berlin Wall.

set up   put together; construct

The bands **set up** their amplifiers near the wall.

1. The cameraman _____ his equipment.

2. They expected to see the concert, but it _____ that the gate was closed.

3. The boy didn't _____ that he knew about the concert.

4. The economic problems _____ a wave of protests.

V.   UNDERSTANDING GRAMMAR: *AFTER*

A.   Read about *after*

After is a subordinating conjunction, which means that it combines a sentence with two clauses.

> **After** years of silence, this was the first protest.

The clause beginning with *after* tells about the event that happened first (the years of silence).

> The two clauses can be reversed with no change in meaning.

> This was the first protest **after years of silence**.

Notice that when the "after" clause comes second, there is no comma between the clauses.

Note: The expression *After that* is a transition expression that comes at the beginning of a clause. It is used to introduce an event that happened later. The word *that* refers to the first event.

> The wall was torn down. **After that**, Germany was a unified country.

B.   Use *after*

Combine the two sentences using after.

1. There were food shortages in many cities. Then, people began to protest.

    _____

2. The wall was torn down in 1989. After that, people began collecting pieces of it.

    _____

3. The wall opened up East Berlin. Then many rock groups had concerts to celebrate.

    _____

4. The Berliners tore down the wall on November 9. Then people from all over came to the site to celebrate.

VI. READ IT AGAIN

Read the article again. Answer the question.

Why was the protest at the rock concert important?

_____

_____

_____

_____

JFK'S INAUGURAL SPEECH

I. PRE-READING

A. Background information

John Fitzgerald Kennedy was the first president of the United States born in the 20th century. He was in office from January of 1961 to November 22, 1963, when he was killed by an assassin. During his short time in office, many important events took place, including the building of the Berlin Wall and the beginning of the Space Race, the African American civil rights movement and the conflict in Vietnam. This famous paragraph is from Kennedy's inaugural address—the speech he gave when he took office as president.

B. Words to know before you read

Find these words in the text. Then match the words to their definitions.

_____ 1. summon	a.	the state of being extremely poor
_____ 2. poverty	b.	partnership
_____ 3. tyranny	c.	create
_____ 4. forge	d.	call
_____ 5. fruitful	e.	oppression
_____ 6. alliance	f.	productive

C. Reading strategy

Read just the first line and the last line, and answer this question.

What is the main idea of this paragraph?

_____

_____

_____

II. READ

Read the text. Mark the words you don't know, but don't stop reading to look them up.

Now the trumpet summons us. . . .[to] a struggle against the common enemies of man: tyranny, poverty, disease, and war itself. Can we forge against these enemies a grand and global alliance, North and South, East and West, that can assure a more fruitful life for all mankind? Will you join in that historic effort? In the long history of the world, only a few generations have been granted the role of defending freedom in its hour of maximum danger. I do not shrink from this responsibility—I welcome it. I do not believe that any of us would exchange places with any other people or any other generation. The energy, the faith, the devotion which we bring to this endeavor will light our country and all who serve it—and the glow from that fire can truly light the world. And so, my fellow Americans: ask not what your country can do for you—ask what you can do for your country. My fellow citizens of the world: ask not what America will do for you, but what together we can do for the freedom of man.

Source: John F. Kennedy Inaugural Address, January 21, 1961

III. COMPREHENSION CHECK

Write the answers to the questions.

1. What are the enemies of man?

    _____

2. Who does Kennedy want in his alliance?

    _____

3. What does he welcome?

    _____

4. What does he want people of the United States to do?

    _____

5. What does he want people of the world to do?

    _____

IV. VOCABULARY BUILDING

A. Understanding from context

Write the word or phrase from the text with the same meaning as the underlined words and phrases.

1. We are being called to <u>fight</u> against the enemies of all people.

    _____

2. Can we create a great <u>partnership</u>?

   _____

3. . . .that can give everyone a <u>better and more productive</u> life. . .

   _____

4. . . .only a few people are <u>given</u> the opportunity to <u>protect</u> our freedom. . .

   _____   _____

5. I do not <u>try to get away from</u> this responsibility.

   _____

6. . . .the <u>dedication</u> we bring to this <u>effort</u>. . .

   _____   _____

7. . . .the <u>light</u> from that fire. . .

   _____

B. Use the new words

Complete the following sentences with these words.

poverty
disease
alliance
assure
grant
devotion
endeavor
glow

1. The two countries formed an _____ to protect their borders.

2. You could see the _____ of the city's lights from far away.

3. The president _____ the people that peace would come soon.

4. In many parts of the world, children go hungry because their families are living in _____.

5. The people were _____ their freedom when the war ended.

6. His _____ to his cause is inspiring.

7. Vaccinations and clean water are used to fight _____.

8. The president is probably sorry that he started this _____.

V. UNDERSTANDING GRAMMAR: EMBEDDED QUESTIONS WITH *CAN*

A. Read about embedded questions

An embedded question is a noun clause that can be introduced by a variety of phrases. An embedded question does not use question word order. Compare these two:

> What **can you do** for your country?
> Ask what **you can do** for your country.

The embedded question uses the subject + *can* + verb word order that is normally found in statements.

If the embedded question does not have a question word, it is introduced with *if*.
> **Can he** help his country?
> I don't know **if he can** help his country.

B. Common phrases to introduce embedded questions

Do you know. . .?

I don't know. . .

I'd like to know. . .

Who knows. . .?

Do you have any idea. . .?

I wonder. . .

I'm not sure. . .

The question is. . .

C. Use embedded questions with *can*

Rewrite the questions as embedded questions. Note that some of them will be statements and some will be questions.

1. How can we win this struggle?

   I don't know _____

2. Can he assure them that they'll be safe?

   I'd like to know_____

3. What benefit can we get from this endeavor?

   I'm not sure _____

4. Can they see the glow from the fireplace?

   I wonder _____

5. Why can't they form an alliance?

   Do you know _____

VI. READ IT AGAIN

Read the speech again. Answer the question.

Kennedy uses "struggle," "historic effort," "this responsibility," and "this endeavor" to refer to the same thing. What is he talking about?

_____

_____

_____

_____

_____

FACING TANKS IN NORTH AFRICA

I. PRE-READING

A. Background information

World War II ended in 1945 but has survived in the public's memory and imagination because of the countless books and movies that have been written about it. This paragraph is from *The Rising Tide*, by well-known historical novelist Jeff Shaara. This part of the book tells the story of soldiers fighting in North Africa. In this scene, the characters are facing German tanks.

B. Words to know before you read

Match the words to their definitions.

_____ 1. halt   a. explosive substance

_____ 2. tank   b. a small device that makes a gun fire

_____ 3. hatch   c. stop

_____ 4. trigger   d. very close to the target

_____ 5. gunpowder   e. a small door on a vehicle or ship

_____ 6. point-blank   f. an armored vehicle

C. Reading strategy

Quickly read the excerpt. Then answer the question.

How many men did he shoot?

_____

II. READ

Read the text. Mark the words you don't know, but don't stop reading to look them up.

They jerked to a halt, and he could see smoke coming from the German tank, waited for the movement, saw it now, the hatch coming open. A think plume of black smoke poured up from inside the tank, and the men appeared, scrambling out, escaping the burning hulk. His hand gripped the trigger of the machine gun, and he watched four men drop to the ground, staggering, wounded, blinded by the smoke and the shattering blast that had ripped into them. He pulled the trigger, sprayed the machine-gun fire back and forth, all four men going down quickly. He paused, took another breath, fought through the stink of gunpowder, saw movement beyond, more tanks, streaks of light. The fight was all around them, tanks and armored cars, perfect confusion, enemies only yards apart, seeking a target in the dust, firing point-blank.

"Move! Ninety degrees starboard! Forward!"

He searched for another target, all four men rising to the battle, all a part of the chaos, a desperate dance of men and machine.

Source: *The Rising Tide*, by Jeff Shaara, New York: Random House, 2006, p. 9.

III. COMPREHENSION CHECK

Mark the sentences T (True) or F (False).

_____ 1. The German soldiers came out of their tank.

_____ 2. He was shooting a rifle.

_____ 3. He killed the German soldiers.

_____ 4. The enemies were near each other.

_____ 5. It was easy to see where to shoot.

_____ 6. The men were dancing.

IV. VOCABULARY BUILDING

A. Understanding from context

Read the phrases. Before you look up words in the dictionary, use the context of the sentence to help you match the verbs with the definitions below.

_____ 1. He **jerked** the door open so quickly that he broke the handle.

_____ 2. The hill was sandy, so they **scrambled** up it on hands and knees.

_____ 3. The soldier **gripped** the gun, afraid that he might drop it.

_____ 4. The man was hurt—he **staggered** slowly along the road.

_____ 5. The gunshot **wounded** the man, but it didn't kill him.

_____ 6. The glass **shattered** when the bullet hit it.

_____ 7. He **ripped** his shirt to make a bandage.

_____ 8. They were **seeking** a way through the enemy line, but they never found one.

    a. move quickly and awkwardly, often using one's hands

    b. look for

    c. hold tightly

    d. break into many pieces

    e. walk unsteadily, as if going to fall

    f. pull suddenly and forcefully

    g. tear

    h. injure, usually in a way that opens the skin

B. Use the new words

Complete the sentences with the bold words from Exercise A.

1. The child _____ his mother's arm so he wouldn't fall.

2. The man was so tired that he _____ down the hallway.

3. The customers who came in the morning were _____ the best deals.

4. He _____ his pants on the fence.

5. That man _____ himself with his own knife.

6. When she dropped the plate, it _____.

7. When they saw the alligator, they _____ out of the river.

8. He _____ on the leash to pull the dog out of the road.

V. UNDERSTANDING GRAMMAR: PARTICIPIAL PHRASES

A. Read about participial phrases

A participle is a verb form ending in *-ed* or *-ing*. Participial phrases are used in many different ways in English—they can be subjects of sentences, they can modify nouns, and they can modify clauses.

In the passage above, the author uses participial phrases to combine clauses. By omitting the verb *be* and using a participle, he gives the writing a more poetic sound. These types of sentences are not common in spoken English.

Look at these comparisons:

*the men appeared, **scrambling out, escaping the burning hulk*** = the men were scrambling out; they were escaping the burning hulk

*he watched four men drop to the ground, **staggering, wounded, blinded*** = the men were staggering, wounded, and blinded

*enemies only yards apart, **seeking a target in the dust, firing point-blank*** = the enemies were seeking a target; they were firing point-blank

In these examples, the participial phrase has the same subject as the main clause. In the following examples, however, the phrase has a new subject:

> ***He*** *. . . sprayed the machine-gun fire back and forth,* **all four men** *going down* = all four men were going down while he sprayed gun fire
> ***He*** *saw it now,* **the hatch** *coming open* = the hatch was coming open when he saw it

B. Identify meaning

Rewrite the participial phrases as separate sentences.

1. The soldiers moved around the building, seeking a safe place to enter.

   _____

2. The commander shouted orders, knowing his men would quickly obey.

   _____

3. The gunfire hit the door, shattering it into a thousand pieces.

   _____

4. He ran into the room, calling orders as he went.

   _____

5. They began the battle, one soldier driving the tank while another used the machine gun.

   _____

VI. READ IT AGAIN

Read the excerpt again. Answer the questions.

1. At the beginning of the excerpt, why do the Germans come out of their tank?

   _____

2. Why does he describe the battle as "chaos"?

   _____

3

San Francisco

CITY TRAVEL TIPS

I. PRE-READING

A. Background information

San Francisco, located in Northern California, is one of the most popular tourist destinations in the United States. The writer of the following article is giving tips for people who want to visit San Francisco. *Tips* are small pieces of advice.

B. Words to know before you read

Match the words to their definitions.

_____ 1. layers   a. a small lake

_____ 2. avoid   b. a boat that carries passengers a short
                                distance

_____ 3. reservation   c. one thing on top of another

_____ 4. ferry   d. an arrangement to save a place for a
                                particular person

_____ 5. pond   e. a bison—a large wild ox native to
                                North America

_____ 6. buffalo   f. stay away from

C. Reading strategy

Skim the following article (read it quickly). Place a check mark by the topics that are covered by the tips.

_____ what to wear

_____ the weather

_____ sports teams

_____ going to restaurants

_____ interesting places to visit

_____ local holidays

_____ public transportation

_____ theater

_____ making conversation

_____ parking

II. READ

Read the text. Mark the words you don't know, but don't stop reading to look them up.

Top 10 Travel Tips for Visiting San Francisco

10. Bring warm clothes, such as sweaters and long pants. However, leave your parka and ski gloves at home. You'll be happier dressing in layers. The average temperature here is about 62° F. Yes, even in the summer.

9. Wear comfortable shoes. You will be doing a lot of walking on steep hills.

8. Avoid the Civic Center (Market and 6th to Market and Van Ness, or thereabouts) after dark. SF has a pretty bad homeless problem in this part of the city. It's getting much better, but there are better places to be at night. Plus, it's rather dirty.

7. Make dinner reservations if you can. In SF, restaurant goers take their food seriously, and you might not be able to get a seat.

6. Take a ride on the ferry. Or rent a bicycle to cross the bridge and visit Sausalito. Maybe pedal on to Tiburon and get the ferry back. There are so many amazing neighborhoods to hang out in that have quirky little restaurants and shops—this is the heart of San Francisco.

5. Be patient with the public transportation. It can be rather good, but confusing as there are two separate tickets you have to buy for BART (subway) and MUNI (buses/streetcars). Do not assume the ticket you bought for BART works on MUNI. There aren't many taxicabs here—hailing one from a street corner is next to impossible—so if you need one, plan ahead and use your cell phone to call for pickup.

4. Visit the parks in this city, especially Golden Gate Park. You could easily spend a week just at this park; there is so much to do. Besides the beautiful walks, there are lakes and ponds you can paddle across or feed the ducks, fields where you can play football with your friends, one of the most incredible museums in the nation (the DeYoung), the Conservatory of Flowers, tennis courts, and even a herd of buffalo!

3. Want to start a conversation? Ask them about their opinion on their city politics. Most San Franciscans know what is going on with their local politics, which are much more active and newsworthy than almost any other city in America.

2. Parking is near impossible. If you get a ticket and leave the United States without paying, you will regret it on your next visit. A 15- to 30-minute search for parking is not uncommon. Budget it into your travel time.

and finally. . .

1. Whatever you do, NEVER EVER call it "Frisco." (Also, please don't call it "San Fran." If you want to abbreviate it, calling it "SF" is the best way to go.)

Source: "Top 10 Travel Tips for Visiting San Francisco," TripAdvisor, http://www.tripadvisor.com/Travel-g60713-c53413/San-Francisco:California:Travel.Tips.html

III. COMPREHENSION CHECK

Mark the sentences T (True) or F (False).

_____ 1. It is extremely cold in San Francisco.

_____ 2. There are many hills in San Francisco.

_____ 3. There are some places tourists should stay away from at night.

_____ 4. The cities of Sausalito and Tiburon are near San Francisco.

_____ 5. Public transportation is terrible in San Francisco.

_____ 6. You can easily call a taxi.

_____ 7. There are animals in Golden Gate Park.

_____ 8. Many San Franciscans are interested in city politics.

_____ 9. It is difficult to park in San Francisco.

_____ 10. Most locals call the city "Frisco."

IV. VOCABULARY BUILDING

A. Understanding from context

Read the sentences. Before you look up words in the dictionary, use the context of the sentence to help you match the boldface words and idioms with the definitions below.

_____ 1. Wear comfortable shoes. You will be doing a lot of walking on **steep** hills.

_____ 2. It's at Market and Van Ness, or **thereabouts**.

_____ 3. Rent a bicycle to cross the bridge and visit Sausalito. Maybe **pedal** on to Tiburon.

_____ 4. There aren't many taxis here—**hailing** one from a street corner is next to impossible.

_____ 5. There are lakes and ponds you can **paddle** across.

_____ 6. There's even a **herd** of buffalo.

_____ 7. Their local politics are much more active and **newsworthy**.

_____ 8. If you get a ticket and leave the United States without paying, you will **regret** it.

   a. ride a bicycle

   b. be sorry about

   c. rising or falling sharply

   d. interesting; topical

   e. in that area

   f. calling

   g. row; use a pole to move a boat across water

   h. a group of animals

B. Use the new words

Complete the sentences with the boldface words from Exercise A.

1. It's difficult to climb the _____ hills.

2. Let's rent a bicycle and _____ through the park.

3. I think it's in Chinatown or _____.

4. She has only seen a _____ of cows in western movies.

5. _____ a taxi is easy in New York but not in San Francisco.

6. I don't know why they're talking about that story on TV. It isn't _____.

7. I didn't visit Golden Gate Park and now I _____ it.

8. The children like to _____ across the lake in a small boat.

C. Learn collocations

Collocations are words that go together. Here are some common noun collocations for four of the adjectives from this article:

steep	*hill; mountain; angle; rise*
unforgettable	*experience; moment; vacation; year*
quirky	*restaurant; personality; person; idea*
local	*politics; news; weather; area*

Complete the sentences using one of the adjectives from the previous list.

1. We had a really _____ vacation last year.

2. He has such a funny, _____ personality!

3. It's a good idea to check the _____ weather before you arrive.

4. There was a _____ rise in prices this year.

5. He follows world news, but he's not that interested in _____ news.

6. Her last year of school was _____.

7. I don't understand all of his _____ ideas.

8. It's difficult to climb a _____ mountain.

V. UNDERSTANDING GRAMMAR: *IF*

A. Read about present and future tense sentences with *if*

A *clause* is a part of a sentence with a subject and a verb. Some sentences have one clause.

> *They make dinner reservations.*

Sentences with *if*, however, contain two clauses, the main clause and the *if* clause.

> <u>Make dinner reservations **if you can**</u>.

B. Tense

Both the *if* clause and the main clause can be in the present tense when you are describing something that is generally true.

> *If people **want** to go to a popular restaurant, they **make** dinner reservations.*

But much of the time, sentences with *if* are talking about the future. In these sentences, a simple present verb is used in the *if* clause.

Note: You cannot use *will* in an *if* clause, even if you have a future meaning.

> *If you **get** a ticket, you **will regret** it.*

C. Punctuation

The main clause and the *if* clause can change orders without changing the meaning of the sentence. However, keep in mind that if the main clause is first, there is no comma. If the *if* clause is first, a comma is necessary.

> *You should plan ahead **if you need a cab**.*

> ***If you need a cab**, you should plan ahead.*

D. Use the grammar: punctuation

Add a comma to these sentences if necessary.

1. If you go to San Francisco be sure to visit Golden Gate Park.

2. You don't need to rent a car if you're going to stay in the city.

3. If you want to visit nearby cities you can take a ferry or BART.

4. If you have children you should visit the Exploratorium.

5. You will have a beautiful view of the bay if you walk across the Golden Gate Bridge.

E. Use the grammar: verb tense

Complete the sentences with the verb in parentheses. Use the present tense, or the future with will, when necessary.

1. If you _____ (visit) San Francisco, you will enjoy yourself.

2. You _____ (see) people from all over the world if you travel around the city.

3. You won't want to go to the park if it _____ (rain).

4. If you want to use public transportation, you _____ (need) to buy two different kinds of tickets.

5. The locals will like it if you _____ (ask) them about city politics.

VI. READ IT AGAIN

Read the tips again. Answer the questions.

1. According to the article, what are three things you should not do while visiting San Francisco?

   _____

   _____

   _____

2. What are two reasons for *not* renting a car when you visit San Francisco?

   _____

   _____

A GUIDE TO CITY NEIGHBORHOODS

I. PRE-READING

A. Background information

The article in this section is also written for visitors to San Francisco. Like most cities, San Francisco has different neighborhoods, each one with its own character. This is a description of three neighborhoods that tourists may want to visit.

B. Words to know before you read

_____ 1. hustle and bustle   a. a painting on a wall

_____ 2. temple   b. an old-fashioned city train car hanging from a cable

_____ 3. boundary   c. one of the first people to explore or settle in a place

_____ 4. railroad baron   d. a lot of activity and noise

_____ 5. cable car   e. building

_____ 6. mural   f. a rich and powerful person in the train
                                    industry

_____ 7. pioneer   g. a place to worship

_____ 8. structure   h. the edge or border

C. Reading strategy

Scan the article for these place-names. Write what each place is famous for on the blanks.

Grant Street _____

Lombard Street _____

Mission Dolores _____

II. READ

Read the text. Mark the words you don't know, but don't stop reading to look them up.

San Francisco Neighborhoods

Chinatown

The entrance to Chinatown at Grant Avenue and Bush Street is called the "Dragon's Gate." Inside are 24 blocks of hustle and bustle, most of it taking place along Grant, the oldest street in San Francisco. This city within a city is best explored on foot; exotic shops, food markets, temples and small museums comprise its boundaries. Visitors can buy herbal remedies, enjoy samples at a tea bar or order a "dim sum" lunch.

Nob Hill

Once the home of the silver kings and railroad barons, the "nabobs," Nob Hill's noble tenants, include Grace Cathedral, a replica of Notre Dame in Paris; the Cable Car Barn, where the cable cars are stored when not in service; and grand hotels. Russian Hill, named for burial sites of Russian hunters who were active in California waters in the early 1800s, is most famous for the sinuous curves of Lombard Street, "the crookedest street in the world," between Hyde and Leavenworth Streets.

Mission District

Boasting some of the best weather in the city, the Mission District, Bernal Heights and Potrero Hill take advantage of an abundance of fog-free days. New restaurants and nightspots are a draw while Mission Dolores, 16th and Dolores Streets, is the oldest structure in San Francisco. Many of the city's pioneers are buried in an adjacent cemetery. The largest concentration of murals in the city adorns buildings, fences and walls throughout the district.

Source: http://www.sanfrancisco.travel/neighborhood/

III. COMPREHENSION CHECK

Write answers to the questions.

1. Where is the Dragon's Gate?

    _____

2. What can you find around the edges of Chinatown?

    _____

3. What does Grace Cathedral look like?

    _____

4. Who was buried on Russian Hill?

    _____

5. How is the weather in the Mission District?

    _____

6. What draws people to the Mission District?

    _____

IV. VOCABULARY BUILDING

A. Classify words

Read the sentences and decide if the boldface words are verbs, nouns, or adjectives. Write each in the correct place in the following chart.

1. He was lucky they found a **remedy** for his illness.
2. The United States **comprises** fifty states.
3. The accident **took place** at 4:00.
4. They don't want to visit the usual places; they want an **exotic** vacation.
5. The little boy **boasted** that he had won the game.
6. She **took advantage of** her free time to relax and read.
7. They never went hungry because there was an **abundance** of food.
8. The **hunter** killed a deer.
9. The courthouse was a beautiful, old, **noble** building.
10. That **replica** of the building looks exactly like the original.
11. The river has so many curves—it's as **sinuous** as a snake.
12. He can't sleep because there is loud machinery in the **adjacent** building.

verb	adjective	noun

B. Use the new words

Write one of the words or phrases from Exercise A next to each definition.

verbs:

1. makes up; constitutes _____

2. talk about oneself with too much pride _____

3. happen _____

4. used _____

adjectives:

5. curvy _____

6. next to _____

7. unusual _____

8. grand _____

nouns:

9. a copy _____

10. a person who kills animals _____

11. a large amount _____

12. a cure _____

V. UNDERSTANDING GRAMMAR

A. Read about superlative adjectives

Review these rules for superlative adjectives:

For most superlatives with one-syllable adjectives, add -est.

old—old*est*

Superlatives for words ending in -y add -iest.

curvy—curv*iest*

Superlatives for other words with two or more syllables use "most."

most famous

These superlatives are irregular:

good—best
bad—worst
far—farthest

Superlatives are often used with *one of the.*

San Francisco is **one of the** *most popular tourist destinations in the United States.*

B. Use the grammar

Complete the sentences with one of the adjectives. Use the superlative form.

steep	large	busy
tall	long	expensive

1. At 853 feet, the Transamerica Pyramid is the _____ building in San Francisco.

2. The Bay Bridge is one of the _____ bridges in the world.

3. Union Square attracts thousands of people—it's the _____ shopping district in the city.

4. French Laundry in San Francisco is one of the _____ restaurants in the United States. It costs about $135 per person.

5. Be careful on Filbert Street. It's one of the _____ streets in San Francisco.

6. Golden Gate Park, the _____ park in San Francisco, is bigger than Central Park in New York.

VI.   READ IT AGAIN

Reread the article, and notice the use of superlatives. Then write one superlative sentence about each neighborhood.

Chinatown: _____

Nob Hill: _____

Mission District: _____

A NEW GOLD RUSH

I.   PRE-READING

A. Background information

In the years 1848 to 1855, around 200,000 people came to California looking for gold. This time frame is now known as the California Gold Rush. Many of these people came to San Francisco, which grew from a town of a few hundred people to a city of around 35,000. You can see evidence of the gold rush history in names throughout California; for example, the state's official nickname is "The Golden State," and the San Francisco professional football team is called "the 49ers," which is what the people looking for gold were called. Although there is not much gold left in California, there are still some people who like to "pan for gold" for fun and relaxation—and sometimes profit. This article is about some people who are out of work and hoping to make a little money panning for gold.

B. Words to know before you read

Match the words to their definitions.

____ 1. prospecting
____ 2. shoveling
____ 3. sifting
____ 4. sorting
____ 5. panning
____ 6. particle

a. wash dirt in a pan to look for gold
b. separating the small pieces using a sieve
c. looking for
d. small piece
e. organizing into categories
f. moving earth with a shovel

C. Reading strategy

These two words are defined in the following text. Scan the story for these words, and write their definitions.

1. sluicer _____

2. garnet _____

II. READ

Read the text. Mark the words you don't know, but don't stop reading to look them up.

New Gold Rush Hits California

DeMello, 60, and his prospecting partner, Mike Gavin, 53, a Los Alamitos roofer idled by the business slowdown, drove 20 miles into the forest north of Azusa, Calif., then hiked up a trail into East Fork Canyon and hopped rocks jutting out of the side of the fast-rushing river, passing trout fishermen, until they found a spot that looked promising. Gavin shoveled furiously along the bank while DeMello sifted and sorted through the dirt.

Reducing his shovel contents to mostly sand, he deposited it slowly into a metal sluicer, a piece of equipment refined but little changed in a century and a half. Placed for river water to run through it, the sluicer catches the heaviest particles in its carpetlike bottom—and the heaviest material is gold. They didn't find enough to buy dinner, but they did get small pieces for their collections.

Downstream, Marc Montelius, 50, of Whittier, was panning and sifting while three friends dug and offered advice from the riverbank. He is a self-employed handyman waiting for an oil refinery job. "I have no illusions of grandeur that I'm going to strike it rich," he said. "It's a good excuse to get out of the house."

He found small pieces of gold and some small garnets, a deep red gemstone. Nothing worth selling, he says.

Source: http://www.usatoday.com/news/offbeat/2009-04-02-goldpanning_N.htm

III. COMPREHENSION CHECK

Mark the sentences T (True) or F (False).

_____ 1. The men in the article are students.

_____ 2. Mike Gavin and Marc Montelius are unemployed.

_____ 3. The men found a lot of gold.

_____ 4. Gold is heavier than sand.

_____ 5. People used sluicers to look for gold 100 years ago.

_____ 6. All three men found small pieces of gold.

IV. VOCABULARY BUILDING

A. Understanding from context

Read the phrases. Before you look up words in the dictionary, use the context of the article to help you circle the letter of the word or phrase with the same meaning as the boldface word.

1. they **hiked** up a trail

   a. walked

   b. ran

2. they **hopped** rocks

   a. fell under rocks

   b. jumped from rock to rock

3. the rocks were **jutting out** of the side of the river

   a. sticking out

   b. near

4. it was a fast-**rushing** river

   a. moving slowly

   b. moving quickly

5. they found a spot that looked **promising**

   a. bad

   b. good

6. a piece of equipment **refined** but little changed in a century
    a. improved
    b. changed

7. he has **illusions** of grandeur
    a. false ideas of greatness
    b. true ideas of greatness

8. he's going to **strike it rich**
    a. hit a rich person
    b. get rich suddenly

B. Use the new words

Complete the sentences with the boldface words and idioms from Exercise A.

1. People buy lottery tickets because they want to _____.

2. This looks like a _____ place for our next vacation.

3. In the mornings everyone is _____ to work.

4. He's a realistic person; he doesn't have any _____.

5. The runner _____ over the low fence.

6. Last summer we _____ up a mountain.

7. He had a sharp nose _____ of his face.

8. They have _____ that computer program so it works perfectly now.

C. Focus on verbs

This article contains many active verbs that make the story more interesting. Without looking at the article, put these verbs into the summary below. When you finish, use the article to check your work.

sorted   sifted   hiked   deposited   hopped   shoveled   looked

First, the men _____ up the mountain. Then they _____ rocks along the river while they _____ for a good spot. One man _____ dirt by the side of the river. The other man _____ the dirt to separate the small particles from the big rocks. After he sifted it, he _____ it into different piles. Once the dirt was mostly small particles of sand, he _____ it into the sluicer.

V. UNDERSTANDING GRAMMAR

A. Read about *while*

We usually use *while* as a conjunction to indicate that two things are happening at the same time.

> Gavin shoveled furiously along the bank **while** DeMello sifted and sorted through the dirt.

Often the past continuous verb form is used with *while* to emphasize that one or more of the actions is ongoing.

> Marc Montelius **was panning and sifting** <u>while</u> three friends dug and offered advice from the riverbank.

While can also be used as a conjunction to indicate a contrast.

> **While** there isn't a lot of gold left in California, there are still many small pieces.
> **While** most prospectors don't find much of value, sometimes one of them gets lucky.

While can also be a noun in the expression *for a while*, meaning "a period of time."

> They waited **for a while**.

> I haven't seen you **for a while**.

B. Use the grammar

Choose the meaning of while as it is used in each sentence. Write the appropriate letters after the sentence.

ST = at the same time

C = contrast

PT = period of time

1. They looked for a while before they found anything. _____
2. He found a garnet while he was looking for gold. _____
3. While finding gold is difficult, searching for it can be entertaining. _____
4. The interviewer spoke to them while they were sifting the sand. _____
5. While there were once thousands of people looking for gold in California, now there are only a few. _____
6. Many 49ers stayed in San Francisco for a while before they went to the mountains. _____

VI.   READ IT AGAIN

Read the article again. Answer the questions.

1.   What are the usual occupations of Mike Gavin and Marc Montelius?

_____

_____

2.   How does a sluicer work?

_____

_____

_____

CAUGHT UP IN THE 1906 EARTHQUAKE

I.   PRE-READING

A. Background information

This reading is from the book *Dragonwings* by Laurence Yep. *Dragonwings* is the story of a young Chinese boy and his father living in San Francisco in the early 1900s. In this part of the story, the boy is experiencing the 1906 earthquake. This terrible earthquake and the fire that followed it destroyed much of the city. It is believed that more than 3,000 people died in the disaster, making it one of the worst in U.S. history.

B. Words to know before you read

_____ 1. tremor

_____ 2. steeple

_____ 3. tenement

_____ 4. surge

_____ 5. topple over

_____ 6. mercifully

a. a tall narrow tower, often the bell tower of a church

b. a house divided into apartments for rent; low-rent housing

c. a movement, sometimes of the earth

d. thankfully

e. move quickly

f. knock over

C. Reading strategy

Skim the following article quickly, and write the answer to the question.

What happened to the tenement house and Miss Whitlaw's fence?

_____

II. READ

Read the text. Mark the words you don't know, but don't stop reading to look them up.

He started to get to his feet when the second tremor shook and he fell forward flat on his face. I heard the city bells ringing. They were rung by no human hand—the earthquake had just shaken them in their steeples. The second tremor was worse than the first. From all over came an immense wall of noise: of metal tearing, of bricks crashing, of wood breaking free from wood nails, and all. Everywhere, what man had built came undone. I was looking at a tenement house to our right and it just seemed to shudder and then collapse. One moment there were solid wooden walls and the next moment it had fallen with the cracking of wood and the tinkling of glass and the screams of people inside.

Mercifully, for a moment, it was lost to view in the cloud of dust that rose up. The debris surged against Miss Whitlaw's fence and toppled it over with a creak and a groan and a crash. I saw an arm sticking up from the mound of rubble and the hand was twisted at an impossible angle from the wrist. Coughing, Father pulled at my arm. "Stay here now," he ordered and started for Miss Whitlaw's.

Source: *Dragonwings*, by Laurence Yep, New York: HarperCollins, 1977.

III. COMPREHENSION CHECK

Read the questions. Circle the best answer.

1. Why did the bells ring?

    a. to warn people about the earthquake

    b. the earthquake shook the bells

2. What did the people do when the tenement house collapsed?

    a. They screamed.

    b. They ran outside.

3. What was making a lot of noise?

    a. dust rising and Father's coughing

    b. metal tearing and bricks crashing

4. Who is in the room with the boy?

    a. Father

    b. Miss Whitlaw

5. Who is Miss Whitlaw?

    a. someone who lives on the other side of the city

    b. someone who lives very nearby

IV. VOCABULARY BUILDING

A. Synonyms

Some of the words in this article have synonyms with very similar meanings. Read the following words and their synonyms. Then complete the sentences with an appropriate word. More than one answer is possible for each sentence. Use the correct form for the verbs.

shudder (v.)	*shake*
collapse (v.)	*fall down*
twist (v.)	*turn*
immense (adj.)	*huge*
debris (n.)	*rubble*
mound (n.)	*pile*

1. The dogs were looking for victims in the _____.

2. There are still some buildings in San Francisco that didn't _____ during the 1906 earthquake.

3. The earthquake caused _____ problems for San Francisco.

4. There was a _____ of clothing on top of the washing machine.

5. Be careful. The road _____ sharply up ahead.

6. The whole house _____ during the earthquake, but it didn't collapse.

7. Many people were injured when the roof _____ on top of them.

8. He hurt his ankle when he _____ it during the earthquake.

9. They put the rocks in large _____ by the side of the road.

10. The economic loss caused by the earthquake was _____.

11. They had to clear the _____ from the old building.

12. People _____ when they are cold or frightened.

V. UNDERSTANDING GRAMMAR

A. Read about the past perfect

The past perfect is formed with *had* + the past participle of a verb. It shows that one action or event happened before another one in the past. It often appears in past tense narratives like this story.

Look at these examples of the past perfect from the story:

*the earthquake **had shaken** them in their steeples*

(The earthquake shook the bells before the boy heard them.)

*what man **had built** came undone*

(Man built the buildings before the earthquake knocked them down.)

the next moment it **had fallen**

(The building was already completely collapsed.)

B. Identify time order

Each sentence contains two verbs. Underline the verb that happened first.

1. He had moved to San Francisco several years before the earthquake hit.

2. They picked up the debris that had fallen during the quake.

3. They helped neighbors that had gotten hurt.

4. They couldn't fight the fire because water pipes had broken in the earthquake.

C. Use the grammar

Complete each sentence with the verbs in parentheses. Put one verb in the simple past and the other verb in the past perfect.

1. He _____ (wake up) early the morning that the earthquake _____ (hit).

2. The people _____ (realize) that they _____ (not prepared) for such a disaster.

3. The fire _____ (destroy) many buildings that _____ (not fall) in the quake.

4. She _____ (go) back to her house, but it _____ (collapse).

5. He _____ (remember) that the building _____ (shudder) violently before it fell down.

VI.   READ IT AGAIN

Read the excerpt again. Answer the questions.

1. What were the houses made of?

   _____

   _____

2. What words does the writer use to describe sounds?

   _____

   _____

   _____

   _____

THE DEVELOPMENT OF ALCATRAZ

I. PRE-READING

A. Background information

Alcatraz Island is right in the middle of beautiful San Francisco Bay and visible from the many high places in the city. These days it seems like a strange place for a prison. However, prisoners of different kinds were held on Alcatraz for over 100 years. The prison closed in 1963, and the island is now a popular tourist destination. These paragraphs tell a small part of Alcatraz's long history.

B. Words to know before you read

_____ 1. fortress

_____ 2. lighthouse

_____ 3. mineral resources

_____ 4. miner

_____ 5. current

_____ 6. captive

_____ 7. capacity

a. prisoner

b. a stream or movement of water

c. amount something can hold

d. useful metals and rocks, like gold and silver

e. a tower with a warning light for ships

f. a person who works to take minerals from the earth

g. a strong, well-protected building or group of buildings

C. Reading strategy

You can learn what period of history is covered by a reading by scanning for dates before you begin. Look quickly for the dates in this reading and write them in order.

_____   _____

_____   _____

_____   _____

_____

II. READ

Read the text. Mark the words you don't know, but don't stop reading to look them up.

By 1853, U.S. Army engineers had started constructing a military fortress on the island, along with the Pacific Coast's first operating lighthouse. In 1848, the discovery of gold along the American River in California brought shiploads of miners from around the world to the West Coast in search of the precious metal. As word spread around the globe of abundant wealth in California, the

United States government would invoke security measures to protect its land and mineral resources from seizure by other countries.

Because of its natural isolation, surrounded by freezing waters and hazardous currents, Alcatraz would soon be considered by the U.S. Army as an ideal location for holding captives. In 1861 the island began receiving Civil War prisoners, and in 1898 the Spanish-American War would bring the prison population from a mere twenty-six to over four hundred and fifty. Then in 1906, following the catastrophic San Francisco earthquake, hundreds of civilian prisoners were transferred to the island for safe confinement. By 1912 a large cell house had been constructed on the island's central crest, and by the late 1920s, the three-story structure was nearly at full capacity.

Source: http://www.alcatrazhistory.com/rs1.htm

III. COMPREHENSION CHECK

These events are not in order. Write the correct date next to each event.

_____ Gold was discovered in California.

_____ The cell house was almost full.

_____ Prisoners from the Spanish-American War came to the island.

_____ The army began building a fortress.

_____ Nonmilitary prisoners were transferred to the prison because of the earthquake.

_____ A three-story prison building was built on the island.

_____ Civil War prisoners started coming to Alcatraz.

IV. VOCABULARY BUILDING

A. Word families

Read the word families in the table. Then choose the correct form for each of the following sentences.

noun	verb	adjective
catastrophe		catastrophic
confinement	confine	confined
abundance		abundant
seizure	seize	
resource		resourceful
hazard		hazardous
isolation	isolate	isolated

1. a. The earthquake was a terrible _____.
    b. The earthquake had _____ results for San Francisco.
2. a. The prisoners were _____ in small cells.
    b. Sometimes their _____ lasted for many years.
    c. The military _____ prisoners of war at Alcatraz.
3. a. People thought that gold was _____ in California.
    b. There was always an _____ of sea birds on the island.
4. a. The government _____ the property of the prisoners.
    b. Wars often start with the _____ of land.
5. a. Gold is a valuable _____.
    b. A _____ person knows how to use the things that are available to him or her.
6. a. Mining was a _____ occupation.
    b. The currents around the island were a _____ for any prisoner who tried to escape.
7. a. Prisoners who broke the rules were _____ for a while.
    b. _____ is very frightening for most people.
    c. Sometimes they _____ a prisoner so he won't hurt other prisoners.

V. UNDERSTANDING GRAMMAR

A. Read about *would*

Would is sometimes used to indicated "future in the past." When the story is a past tense narrative, *would* can show that one event was future to another.

Read these examples based on the story about Alcatraz:

As word spread around the globe of wealth in California, the United States government *would invoke* security measures to protect its land. (First, the word spread. Then the government invoked security measures.)

Alcatraz *would* soon *be considered* by the U.S. Army as an ideal location for holding captives. (First, Alcatraz was discovered. Then it was considered an ideal place for captives.)

In 1898 the Spanish-American War *would bring* the prison population from a mere twenty-six to over four hundred and fifty. (First, there were 26 prisoners. Then the Spanish-American War brought the population to 450.)

B. Use the grammar

Complete these sentences with an appropriate verb. Use would + verb *to show future-in-the-past.*

1. When the prisoners came to the island, they knew they _____ there for many years.

2. The family moved to San Francisco without knowing that an immense earthquake _____ the next year.

3. After the 1930s, as many as 300 prisoners _____ at Alcatraz.

4. At that time, they didn't know the prison _____ in 1963.

VI. READ IT AGAIN

Read the article again. Answer the questions.

1. Why was Alcatraz a good place for a prison?

   _____

2. Which wars caused prisoners to be sent to Alcatraz?

   _____

The Early United States

CIVIL WAR REENACTMENT

I. PRE-READING

A. Background information

Reenactment is a popular hobby all over the United States. In a reenactment, people dress in costumes from a particular time period and act out a historical event, often a battle. The Civil War (1861–1865) is the most popular era, but there are also many reenactments of the Revolutionary War (1775–1783), when the American colonies broke free of British rule. This newspaper article is about a reenactment that takes place every year in South Carolina.

B. Words to know before you read

Match the words to their definitions.

_____ 1. musket   a. a guard

_____ 2. backcountry   b. a long gun that shot lead balls

_____ 3. militia   c. a fight

_____ 4. trounce   d. an army of regular citizens (not trained soldiers)

_____ 5. battle   e. an area far from the city

_____ 6. skirmish   f. defeat

_____ 7. sentry   g. a small battle

C. Reading strategy

Scan this story for names and numbers. Then answer the questions.

1. Where did the event take place? _____

2. What day? _____

3. What time? _____

II. READ

Read the text. Mark the words you don't know, but don't stop reading to look them up.

Battle of Huck's Defeat hasn't lost authenticity

Annual Brattonsville reenactment is riveting for spectators
by Kathy Haight khaight@charlotteobserver.com
Posted: Sunday, July 10, 2011

The sound of musket fire in a York County field Saturday took visitors back to 1780—when the tide of the American Revolution began turning toward the Patriots.

At the Brattonsville historic site, 18 men dressed as a backcountry militia trounced the Redcoats in the annual re-enactment of the Battle of Huck's Defeat.

"The British thought they had won the war when they captured Charleston," said historian Michael Scoggins of York County's Culture & Heritage Museums. "It was here in the backcountry that they found out different."

The skirmish was part of a weekend of events at Historic Brattonsville, a collection of homes, farm buildings and gardens about 35 miles southwest of Charlotte. The re-enactment of another battle is scheduled for 2 p.m. today.

As Saturday's action got under way, shots rang out from the woods near a house surrounded by British soldiers. A sentry in a red wool vest and canvas leggings fell dead in a field near the house, while several hundred visitors wearing shorts and T-shirts looked on. Soon the field was full of 18th-century smoke and muskets being recorded digitally by 21st-century cameras.

"It feels like I'm going back in time," said Dennis Marcone, 46, of Charlotte, who got hooked on history because that's the subject his father taught. He likes watching re-enactments because they immerse him in the past as if he was really there.

Source: http://www.charlotteobserver.com/2011/07/10/2442705/battle-of-hucks-defeat-hasnt-lost.html#ixzz1SZPZUMBK

III. COMPREHENSION CHECK

Write the answer to the questions.

1. What is the name of the battle?

   _____

2. What is Historic Brattonsville?

   _____

3. How many men were dressed as American militia?

   _____

4. What was the British guard wearing?

    _____

5. What does "immerse him in the past" mean?

    _____

IV. VOCABULARY BUILDING

A. Idioms and two-word verbs

Read the expressions and their definitions. Then answer the following questions.

get under way	*begin*
take [someone] back	*remind someone of the past*
turn the tide	*cause the circumstances to reverse*
get hooked on	*get addicted to*
go back in time	*travel to the past*
look on	*watch an event without participating*
find out	*discover information*

1. What reminded the visitors of 1780?

    _____

2. Who feels like he is traveling to the past?

    _____

3. What were the people watching the reenactment wearing?

    _____

4. Why did Dennis Marcone get addicted to history?

    _____

5. When did the circumstances of the Revolution start to reverse?

    _____

6. Where did the British discover that they hadn't won the war?

    _____

7. What happened as the reenactment began?

    _____

B. Use the vocabulary

Complete the sentences using the expressions from Part A. Use the correct verb form.

1. The crowd of people _____ as the men fought.

2. She _____ that TV show last year. Now she watches it every week.

3. The demonstration _____ at 10:00 and finished at 12:15.

4. They arrived at 4:00 and _____ that they had missed the reenactment.

5. Looking at those photos _____ to my childhood.

6. They were losing the war until that battle _____.

V. UNDERSTANDING GRAMMAR

A. Read about *as if*

As if is used to express what a situation seems like. Look at this sentence:

> The reenactments immerse him in the past *as if he was really there.*

Using the past tense after *as if* indicates that the situation is unreal.

> He spends money **as if** he **had** *a million dollars.* (He doesn't have a million dollars.)
> They fight **as if** they **were** *going to win.* (They are not going to win.)

The present tense can also be used after *as if* to indicate that the statement might be true.

> He spends money **as if** he **has** *a million dollars.* (Maybe he has a million dollars.)
> They fight **as if** they **are** *going to win.* (It seems like they are going to win.)

As though has the same meaning as *as if*.

Note: Don't confuse *as if* with *as*. *As* means *while*—at the same time. For example:

> As Saturday's action got under way, shots rang out from the woods.

As can appear at the beginning of a sentence or in the middle.

> Shots rang out as Saturday's action got under way.

As if doesn't usually appear at the beginning of a sentence.

B. Use the grammar

Complete the sentences with as *or* as if.

1. _____ they fought, the sky filled with smoke.

2. He fell down _____ he had been shot.

3. They dressed _____ they lived in the 18th century.

4. The people watched _____ the fighting got more intense.

5. The militia prepared their defense _____ the Redcoats surrounded the building.

6. It sounds _____ there was a real battle going on.

VI.   READ IT AGAIN

Read the story again. Answer the question.

Why was the Battle of Huck's Defeat important?

_____

"PAUL REVERE'S RIDE"

I.   PRE-READING

A. Background information

The night before the first battles of the American Revolution, Paul Revere rode through Middlesex County in Massachusetts to warn the colonists that the British army was coming. The colonists were prepared for the British, and they won this first battle. Revere was not the only rider that night, but everyone knows his name because of this poem about his ride. It was written in 1861 by the famous poet Henry Wadsworth Longfellow. It is a long poem—the lines here are from the beginning and near the end.

B. Words to know before you read

lantern	*light*
aloft	*up high*
belfry	*bell tower*
signal	*something that gives information*
to arm	*to get weapons*
shore	*the side of a river*

Look at the previous definitions. Write the meaning of these lines:

Hang a lantern aloft in the belfry arch
Of the North Church tower as a signal light

_____

_____

C. Reading strategy

This poem uses rhyme—words that have the same sound—at the end of each line. In many cases, the rhymes are in pairs called "rhyming couplets" as in the first two lines, which rhyme *hear* and *Revere*.

In the following poem, look through the words at the end of each line. Which lines are rhyming couplets? On the following blanks, write the line numbers and the rhyming words. (In one case, there are three rhyming lines together.)

Example:

lines 1 and 2, hear/Revere

_____

_____

_____

_____

_____

_____

_____

_____

II. READ

Read the text. Mark the words you don't know, but don't stop reading to look them up.

"Paul Revere's Ride"

by Henry Wadsworth Longfellow

1 Listen my children and you shall hear
   Of the midnight ride of Paul Revere,
   On the eighteenth of April, in Seventy-five;
   Hardly a man is now alive
   Who remembers that famous day and year.

6 He said to his friend, "If the British march
   By land or sea from the town to-night,
   Hang a lantern aloft in the belfry arch
   Of the North Church tower as a signal light,—
   One if by land, and two if by sea;

11 And I on the opposite shore will be,
Ready to ride and spread the alarm
Through every Middlesex village and farm,
For the country folk to be up and to arm."

----

110 You know the rest. In the books you have read
How the British Regulars fired and fled,—
How the farmers gave them ball for ball,
From behind each fence and farmyard wall,
Chasing the redcoats down the lane,
Then crossing the fields to emerge again

116 Under the trees at the turn of the road,
And only pausing to fire and load.
So through the night rode Paul Revere;
And so through the night went his cry of alarm
To every Middlesex village and farm,—

121 A cry of defiance, and not of fear,
A voice in the darkness, a knock at the door,
And a word that shall echo for evermore!

III. COMPREHENSION CHECK

Write the answers to the questions.

1. What was the date of Paul Revere's ride?

   _____

2. The British came in ships. How many lanterns did Revere's friend hang in the church tower?

   _____

3. What did Revere tell the people to do?

   _____

4. Where did the farmers stand while they were shooting?

   _____

IV. VOCABULARY BUILDING

Read the words and the definitions. Both definitions are possible for each word. Use the context of the poem to help you decide which meaning of the word defines its use in the poem.

1. shore

   a. to support or hold up

   b. the land at the edge of a river

2. spread

    a. to cause something to reach more and more people

    b. to make something bigger by extending it

3. fire

    a. to shoot a gun

    b. to dismiss an employee

4. load

    a. to put ammunition in a gun

    b. to put things in a vehicle

5. chase

    a. to run after in order to catch

    b. to seek the company of someone of the opposite sex

6. pause

    a. to stop temporarily

    b. to interrupt the operation of a recording device

7. echo

    a. to express agreement

    b. to continue to have significance

8. emerge

    a. to come out (as information)

    b. to come into view

V. UNDERSTANDING GRAMMAR

A. Read about *hardly*

Hardly is an adverb with several closely related meanings.

It can mean *almost not* or *almost none*, particularly when used with *ever* or *any*.

> We **hardly ever** visit them.
> There were **hardly any** people left.

This meaning is used in the poem:

> **Hardly** a man is still alive. . .

It can also mean *just*.

> The people had **hardly** arrived when the battle started.

Because this meaning deals with time, it is often used with the conjunction *when*.

Because the meaning of *hardly* is negative, in standard English it is not used in negative sentences. (Double negatives are normally avoided.)

Note: *Hardly* is not the adverb for *hard*. *Hard* can be an adjective or an adverb.

> That was **hard** work.
> He works **hard**.

The adverbs *scarcely* and *barely* are very close in meaning to *hardly*.

Rewrite or combine the sentences using hardly.

Examples:

He had spread the alarm. The British came right away.
He had hardly spread the alarm when the British came.

There were almost no chairs in the room.
There were hardly any chairs in the room.

1. We almost never go to the movies.

   _____

2. He had just loaded the gun. Then he had to fire.

   _____

3. He closed the book. He fell asleep immediately.

   _____

4. There were almost no professional soldiers in the army.

   _____

5. They almost never spoke about the problem.

   _____

VI. READ IT AGAIN

Read the poem again. Answer the questions.

1. What two names are used for the British army?

   _____

2. Why does Longfellow say that Paul Revere's word would "echo for evermore"?

   _____

THE DECLARATION OF INDEPENDENCE

I. PRE-READING

A. Background information

The U.S. Declaration of Independence was adopted on July 4, 1776. This document, written primarily by Thomas Jefferson, explains why the United States declared independence from Great Britain. The excerpt here contains the most famous lines from the Declaration.

B. Words to know before you read

_____ 1. self-evident

_____ 2. endowed

_____ 3. unalienable*

_____ 4. end

_____ 5. alter

_____ 6. abolish

_____ 7. derive

_____ 8. foundation

a. change

b. eliminate

c. basis

d. given

e. goal

f. come from

g. clear; obvious

h. something that cannot be taken away

*This word was used in the Declaration of Independence, but the more usual form is "inalienable." It's almost always used to describe rights.

C. Reading strategy

At the time this was written, English did not have the modern rules for capitalization. Writers often capitalized words they felt were important. Look through the text quickly. Write the words and phrases that are capitalized here but wouldn't be in a modern text.

_____   _____

_____   _____

_____   _____

_____   _____

_____   _____

II. READ

Read the text. Mark the words you don't know, but don't stop reading to look them up.

We hold these truths to be self-evident, that all men are created equal, that they are endowed by their Creator with certain unalienable Rights, that among these are Life, Liberty and the pursuit of Happiness.—That to secure these rights, Governments are instituted among Men, deriving their just powers from the consent of the governed,—That whenever any Form of Government becomes destructive of these ends, it is the Right of the People to alter or to abolish it, and to institute new Government, laying its foundation on such principles and organizing its powers in such form, as to them shall seem most likely to effect their Safety and Happiness.

III. COMPREHENSION CHECK

Circle the letter of the phrases with the same meaning.

1. We hold these truths to be self-evident, that all men are created equal. . .

    a. We believe that it's clear that all men are created equal.

    b. We can provide evidence that all men are created equal.

2. . . .that they are endowed by their Creator with certain unalienable Rights. . .

    a. that God has rights that cannot be taken away

    b. that God has given men rights that cannot be taken away

3. . . .Governments are instituted among Men, deriving their just powers from the consent of the governed. . .

    a. Governments have power because the people agree to give it to them.

    b. Governments can take power from the people they govern.

4. . . .That whenever any Form of Government becomes destructive of these ends, it is the Right of the People to alter or to abolish it. . .

    a. People have the right to change or eliminate any government.

    b. People have the right to change or eliminate government that takes away their rights.

5. . . .institute new Government, laying its foundation on such principles and organizing its powers in such form, as to them shall seem most likely to effect their Safety and Happiness.

    a. create a new government based on these ideas and set up in a way that will allow people to be safe and happy

    b. create a new government based on these ideas and set up in a way that is destructive to safety and happiness

IV. VOCABULARY BUILDING

A. Word families

Read the word families in the chart.

noun	verb	adjective
alteration	alter	
creation/creator	create	creative
destruction	destroy	destructive
equality		equal
evidence		evident
happiness		happy
institution	institute	
safety		safe

B. Use the new words

Complete the sentences with words from the chart in Part A. Use appropriate verb forms.

1. **a.** He made several _____ to the document before he printed it.

    b. They _____ the coat so it would fit a smaller person.

2. **a.** The artist _____ several beautiful works.

    b. He is very proud of his _____.

    c. Everyone wanted to speak to the _____ of the work.

3. **a.** The war _____ the city.

    b. The _____ was terrible.

    c. The weapons were very _____.

4. **a.** We were guaranteed _____ treatment.

    b. The people fought for _____.

5. **a.** He presented _____ to support his argument.

    b. The truth of his statement was _____.

6. **a.** They were _____ about the changes.

    b. The end of the war brought _____ to the people.

7. **a.** We need to _____ some changes around here.

    b. That bank is a wealthy _____.

8. **a.** A government's first concern is the _____
of its people.

    b. The colonists didn't feel _____ because
they didn't have rights.

V. UNDERSTANDING GRAMMAR

A. Read about *that* clauses after mental activity verbs

Some verbs are often followed by a noun clause beginning with *that*. A noun
clause always contains a subject and a verb.

    *We believe **that** all men are created equal.*

Many of the verbs commonly followed by noun clauses are "mental activity"
verbs—they describe things that are happening in our minds. They include:

- agree
- assume
- believe
- decide
- discover
- guess
- hope
- know
- learn
- notice
- predict
- prove
- realize
- think
- understand

While speaking, it is possible to omit *that* from sentences with noun clauses,
but it is often included in writing.

*Use verbs from the previous word list to complete the sentences. Be sure to use
the correct verb forms. More than one answer may be possible.*

1. Columbus _____ that he would reach Asia by sailing west.

2. He didn't _____ that he wasn't in Asia.

3. Paul Revere _____ that the British were coming by sea.

4. The colonists _____ that they had to declare independence.

5. Everyone _____ that war wouldn't last long.

VI. READ IT AGAIN

Read the excerpt again. Answer the question.

What rights are mentioned in the text?

_____

CHRISTOPHER COLUMBUS' JOURNAL

I. PRE-READING

A. Background information

Christopher Columbus left Spain on his first journey to the New World in 1492. He returned to Spain in 1493 thinking that he had traveled to Asia. During the voyage, he kept a journal describing the places and people he saw. This excerpt tells about his meeting with native people in the Caribbean. Columbus never came to the land that is now the United States, but his voyages showed other Europeans how to get to the Americas.

B. Words to know before you read

The following words from this text are not very common:

wrought	*made of or shaped from.* This meaning is archaic (not used in modern English).
javelin	*a light spear*
strove	*past tense of* strive, *which means try or make an effort.* Strive is used today, as in *We strive for success*, but this irregular past tense form is not common.
vessel	*a container.* This word is more commonly used now to mean *ship* or *boat.*
baker's peel	*a flat shovel-like tool that bakers use to transfer loaves of bread or pizzas into or out of an oven.*
calabash	*a water container*

C. Reading strategy

Read the first sentence and the last sentence in the following text. Then answer the questions.

1. How did the native people come to the ship?

_____

2. What did Columbus learn from the natives?

_____

II. READ

Read the text. Mark the words you don't know, but don't stop reading to look them up.

Christopher Columbus' Journal

They came to the ship in canoes, made of a single trunk of a tree, wrought in a wonderful manner considering the country; some of them large enough to contain forty or forty-five men, others of different sizes down to those fitted to hold but a single person. They rowed with an oar like a baker's peel, and wonderfully swift. If they happen to upset, they all jump into the sea, and swim 'til they have righted their canoe and emptied it with the calabashes they carry with them. They came loaded with balls of cotton, parrots, javelins, and other things too numerous to mention; these they exchanged for whatever we chose to give them. I was very attentive to them, and strove to learn if they had any gold. Seeing some of them with little bits of this metal hanging at their noses, I gathered from them by signs that by going southward or steering round the island in that direction, there would be found a king who possessed large vessels of gold, and in great quantities.

III. COMPREHENSION CHECK

Select the correct answer from the passage.

1. What were the canoes made of?

    a. gold

    b. cotton

    c. a tree trunk

2. How many people did the smallest canoe hold?

    a. one

    b. forty

    c. forty-five

3. What did they use the calabashes for?

    a. for trading

    b. for taking water out of the canoes

    c. for carrying gold

4. Which thing did they carry in the canoes?

    a. gold

    b. baker's peels

    c. birds

5. What did they wear on their faces?

    a. metal bars

    b. a large amount of gold

    c. a small amount of gold

IV. VOCABULARY BUILDING

A. Classify words

Find these words in the text, and decide if they are used as verbs or nouns. Write them in the correct place in the following chart.

canoe

oar

row

empty

cotton

parrot

steer

right

gather

trunk

upset

quantity

verb	noun

B. Use the vocabulary

Complete the sentences with the words from Part A. Use the correct verb forms, and make nouns plural if necessary.

1. He used an _____ to move the boat forward in the water.

2. Some _____ know how to talk.

3. To _____ something is to knock it over.

4. They _____ the boat through rough water.

5. He _____ a lot of information from the men.

6. The boat was made from a large tree _____.

7. They had to _____ the boat because it was full of water.

8. They had to _____ the boat because it turned over.

9. They knew how to _____ very quickly with those oars.

10. A _____ is long, thin boat.

11. The _____ plant became an important source of fabric.

12. They had a large _____ of items to exchange.

V. UNDERSTANDING GRAMMAR

A. Read about *until*

'Til is short for *until* and has the same meaning. It can be followed by a noun.

> *They waited **until** ['til] dark.*

It can also be followed by a clause.

> *They all jump in the sea and swim 'til [until] they have righted it again.*

Note: *Until* is only used to refer to time. Don't use it for distance or quantity. For example, *They sailed until the Caribbean* and *I counted until 30* are **not** correct. These sentences require *up to*.

> *Until* means up to a certain point in time—and not beyond. The sentence *I'm home until 6:00* means that I will not be home after 6:00.

B. Use the grammar

Write a sentence about each situation, using until.

Example:

They stayed on the island. They left when they ran out of food.

<u>*They stayed on the island until they ran out of food*</u>.

1. They traded with the visitors. The visitors left.

   _____

2. He explored the Caribbean. He left when it was time to go home.

   _____

3. They worked on the building. They stopped at midnight.

_____

4. They continued searching for gold in the New World. Eventually, they died.

_____

VI.   READ IT AGAIN

Read the journal entry again. Answer the question.

What did the natives want in exchange for the things they brought?

_____

5

Entertainment

THE MAIN MOVIE GENRES

I. PRE-READING

A. Background information

A *genre* is a category, usually of literature, film, or television. The following descriptions come from a list of genre descriptions on the website www .filmsite.org. The website contains a huge amount of information about movies of all kinds.

B. Words to know before you read

Match the words to their definitions.

_____ 1. stunt	a. causing emotional release
_____ 2. two-dimensional	b. bad guy
_____ 3. escapism	c. focusing on the story
_____ 4. plot-driven	d. part of a larger group
_____ 5. subsets	e. not complex or deep
_____ 6. cathartic	f. a skillful action (especially in a movie)
_____ 7. quest	g. distraction from reality
_____ 8. villain	h. search

C. Reading strategy

Quickly read the first line of each paragraph. Then answer the question.

What four genres are described here?

_____

_____

_____

_____

II. READ

Read the text. Mark the words you don't know, but don't stop reading to look them up.

Main Film Genres

Action films usually include high energy, big-budget physical stunts and chases, possibly with rescues, battles, fights, escapes, destructive crises (floods, explosions, natural disasters, fires, etc.), non-stop motion, spectacular rhythm and pacing, and adventurous, often two-dimensional "good-guy" heroes (or recently, heroines) battling "bad guys"—all designed for pure audience escapism.

Dramas are serious, plot-driven presentations, portraying realistic characters, settings, life situations, and stories involving intense character development and interaction. Usually, they are not focused on special-effects, comedy, or action. Dramatic films are probably the largest film genre, with many subsets.

Horror films are designed to frighten and to invoke our hidden worst fears, often in a terrifying, shocking finale, while captivating and entertaining us at the same time in a cathartic experience. Horror films feature a wide range of styles, from the earliest silent Nosferatu classic, to today's CGI monsters and deranged humans.

Sci-fi films are often quasi-scientific, visionary and imaginative—complete with heroes, aliens, distant planets, impossible quests, improbable settings, fantastic places, great dark and shadowy villains, futuristic technology, unknown and unknowable forces, and extraordinary monsters ("things or creatures from space"), either created by mad scientists or by nuclear havoc. Science fiction often expresses the potential of technology to destroy humankind and easily overlaps with horror films.

Source: http://www.filmsite.org/genres.html
written by Tim Dirks

III. COMPREHENSION CHECK

Mark the sentences T (True) or F (False).

_____ 1. Action films usually have some expensive scenes.

_____ 2. Action films move quickly.

_____ 3. Action films have complex characters.

_____ 4. Action films usually make the audience think.

_____ 5. Dramas often have two-dimensional characters.

_____ 6. Dramas focus mainly on the story.

_____ 7. Special effects are usually important in dramas.

_____ 8. There are probably more dramas than other kinds of films.

_____ 9. Horror films can provide emotional release.

_____ 10. There are only a few styles of horror movies.

_____ 11. Science fiction films often deal with monsters, space travel, or technology.

_____ 12. Some science fiction films are also horror films.

IV. VOCABULARY BUILDING

A. Classify words

Find these words in the text, and decide if they are nouns, verbs, or adjectives. Write them in the correct places in the following chart.

crises

range

captivate

deranged

improbable

rhythm

havoc

overlap

nouns	verbs	adjectives

B. Identify meaning

Write words from the chart that can replace the underlined words.

1. There are many movies about the <u>destruction</u> caused by nuclear war.

   _____

2. Many horror movies feature an <u>insane</u> killer.

   _____

3. Often science fiction movies are set in <u>unlikely</u> worlds.

   _____

4. There is a wide <u>variety</u> of styles within each genre.

   _____

5. Adventure movies often show <u>terrible things</u> happening.

   _____

6. A good movie will always <u>hold the attention of</u> the audience.

   _____

7. The <u>tempo</u> of an action movie is usually fast and exciting.

   _____

8. Many films fit more than one genre; for example, action, horror, and drama can all <u>occur together</u> in a science fiction movie.

   _____

V. UNDERSTANDING GRAMMAR: FROM VERB TO ADJECTIVE WITH *-ABLE*

A. Read about adjectives with *-able*

One very common adjective ending is *-able*, meaning "can." These adjectives are often (but not always) formed from verbs; for example, *knowable* is something that can be known, and *believable* is something that can be believed.

   Here are a few examples of verbs that are commonly turned into adjectives with the *-able* ending:

adjust

adore

advise

climb

control

debate

dispose

do

excite

live

microwave

recognize

B. Use the grammar

Rewrite the sentences using an adjective with -able. Remember that the final -e is removed when you add -able to a verb (adore—adorable).

1. This old house is really a place you can live.

    _____

2. They told the hero that the mountain could not be climbed.

    _____

3. Some small dogs are very easy to excite.

    _____

4. That point is something we can debate.

    _____

5. She likes to buy the popcorn that can be microwaved.

    _____

6. When he cut his hair and grew a beard, he couldn't be recognized anymore.

    _____

VI. READ IT AGAIN

Read the genre paragraphs again. Answer the questions.

1. Which two kinds of film often focus on heroes and villians?

    _____

2. How is drama different from the other three genres?

    _____

REVIEWS FOR *TITANIC*

I. PRE-READING

A. Background information

The following paragraphs are from reviews of the movie *Titanic* in 1997. *Titanic* made the most money of any film up to that time. It held that record for twelve years, until *Avatar*, a movie by the same director, James Cameron, broke the record in 2009. *Titanic* was rereleased in 3-D in 2012.

B. Words to know before you read

Match the words to their definitions.

____ 1. spellbinding		a.	unforgivable
____ 2. epic		b.	perfectly
____ 3. drift		c.	not affected; left with no feeling
____ 4. astound		d.	fascinating
____ 5. flawlessly		e.	a grand, heroic story
____ 6. untouched		f.	slow movement
____ 7. unpardonable		g.	amaze

C. Reading strategy

Quickly read the following reviews. Which critic didn't like the movie?

a. Ebert

b. Kellen

c. Howe

II. READ

Read the text. Mark the words you don't know, but don't stop reading to look them up.

Titanic

"James Cameron's 194-minute, $200 million film of the tragic voyage is in the tradition of the great Hollywood epics. It is flawlessly crafted, intelligently constructed, strongly acted and spellbinding. If its story stays well within the traditional formulas for such pictures, well, you don't choose the most expensive film ever made as your opportunity to reinvent the wheel."

—Roger Ebert

Source: http://rogerebert.suntimes.com/apps/pbcs.dll/article?AID=/19971219/
REVIEWS/712190303/1023

"Extravagant, exhilarating, devastating, poetic, romantic and totally unforgettable, *Titanic* is an extraordinary achievement in film making, where technology astounds, yet the human story shines even brighter."

—Louise Keller

Source: http://www.urbancinefile.com.au/home/view.asp?a=678&s=Reviews

"'Titanic' is a good, often stunning movie caught in a three-and-a-half hour drift. As we marvel at the physical spectacle of the *Titanic*'s last few hours, we're left staggeringly untouched by the people facing their last moments. This movie should have blown us out of the water. Instead we catch ourselves occasionally thinking the unpardonable thought: 'OK, sink already.'"

—Desson Howe

Source: http://www.washingtonpost.com/wp-srv/style/longterm/movies/videos/titanichowe.htm

III. COMPREHENSION CHECK

Mark the sentences (T) True or (F) False.

_____ 1. Ebert liked the acting.

_____ 2. Ebert thought the story was original and different.

_____ 3. Keller thought the technology in the film was amazing.

_____ 4. Keller liked the romantic story.

_____ 5. Howe was interested in the characters in the story.

_____ 6. Howe thought the movie was too long.

IV. VOCABULARY BUILDING

A. Classify words

Read the adjectives and nouns in the chart. Find and underline one of the forms in the text. Then complete the following sentences with either the noun or adjective form.

nouns	adjectives
flaw	flawless
intelligence	intelligent
tradition	traditional
extravagance	extravagant
exhilaration	exhilarating
romance	romantic
poem	poetic

1. **a.** The story is about a _____ between a rich woman and a poor artist.

   b. Many people think the story is very _____.

2. **a.** The love story in the movie is not surprising; it's a _____ story that we have heard before.

   b. There is a long _____ in the movies of including a love story in historical dramas.

3. **a.** The rich people on the ship had beautiful clothes and fine food and every _____.

   b. The passengers were amazed by the beautiful, _____ _____ dining room on the *Titanic*.

4. **a.** The scene of the couple standing at the front of the ship showed the _____ of freedom and young love.

   b. Standing at the front of the huge ship with their arms out was a very _____ feeling for the young couple.

5. **a.** It turned out that the ship was not as perfect as everyone thought; there were some important _____.

   b. It turned out that the ship was not as _____ as they thought.

6. **a.** Many _____ have been written about the sinking of the *Titanic*.

   b. The movie explores a _____ side of the terrible tragedy.

7. **a.** Ebert feels that Cameron put the story together in an _____ way.

   b. Ebert feels that Cameron constructed the story with _____.

B. Idioms

Read the sentences. Use the context of the sentence to help you match the boldface idioms with the definitions that follow.

_____ 1. If its story stays well within the traditional formulas for such pictures, well, you don't choose the most expensive film ever made as your opportunity to **reinvent the wheel**.

_____ 2. The technology astounds, yet the human story **shines** even **brighter**.

_____ 3. This movie should have **blown us out of the water**. Instead we catch ourselves occasionally thinking the unpardonable thought: "OK, sink already."
   a. amazed us
   b. try to create something that has already been done before
   c. is more beautiful or more interesting

V. UNDERSTANDING GRAMMAR: ADVERBS OF MANNER

<u>A.</u> Read about adverbs of manner

Adverbs of manner describe how something is done.

flawlessly	*crafted*
intelligently	*constructed*
strongly	*acted*

Adverbs of manner are usually placed after the main verb.

*She sang **beautifully**.*

If the verb has a direct object, the adverb comes after the object.

*She sang the music **beautifully**.*

When adverbs of manner describe participles, they can come before the participle.

*The music was **beautifully** sung.*

Here are twenty common adverbs of manner ending in -ly:

badly

beautifully

carefully

cheerfully

clearly

closely

correctly

easily

enormously

faithfully

generously

happily

innocently

kindly

loudly

politely

quietly

regularly

sadly

softly

B. Use adverbs of manner

Rewrite each sentence. Add the adverb of manner.

1. The young man said hello. (cheerfully)

2. The owners inspected the ship. (closely)

3. The older man spoke to the young woman. (kindly)

4. The story was told by the old woman. (sadly)

5. The ship was reproduced by the director. (faithfully)

6. The movie did not end. (happily)

VI. READ IT AGAIN

Read the reviews again. Answer the questions.

1. All of the reviewers use words to describe *Titanic* that mean "amazing" or "interesting." Write one of those words from each review.

2. Keller and Howe don't use the words "special effects," but they both suggest that the special effects of *Titanic* were excellent. Write a phrase from each review that suggests the special effects were good.

FROM NORMA JEANE TO MARILYN MONROE

I. PRE-READING

A. Background information

The following paragraphs are from the biography *Marilyn Monroe* by Barbara Leaming. Monroe was an actress and famous sex symbol in the 1950s. Her blond "look" is so well known and has been copied so many times that most people today still recognize her face, even if they have never seen her movies.

Marilyn Monroe was born with the name Norma Jeane Baker, and she had a very difficult childhood and dreamed of escaping to Hollywood. At 16 years old, she married Jimmy Dougherty, a 21-year-old neighbor. This passage tells the story of how Norma got started on her road to Hollywood fame.

B. Words to know before you read

Match the words to their definitions.

____ 1. ship out		a.	make active again
____ 2. defense factory		b.	free time for a sailor
____ 3. corporal		c.	to leave for a military job
____ 4. reactivate		d.	film of an actor done to see if he/she is good for a role
____ 5. shore leave		e.	a place where military weapons are made
____ 6. screen test		f.	a low-level officer in the military

C. Reading strategy

Quickly scan the first paragraph for years and words with capital letters. Then answer the questions.

1. What years are mentioned in this paragraph? _____

2. What important world event was happening at that time?

   _____

II. READ

Read the text. Mark the words you don't know, but don't stop reading to look them up.

Norma Jeane might well have remained a housewife in the San Fernando Valley for the rest of her life if World War II had not intervened. The young husband left his job at the Lockheed aircraft factory to join the Merchant Marine. In spring 1944, he shipped out. Like many wartime wives, Norma Jeane went to live with her husband's parents and found a job in a defense factory.

In 1945 Army photographers from the First Motion Picture Unit came to Radio Plane to film women in war work. A young corporal named David Conover spotted Norma Jeane and took her picture. When the results came back from the lab, Conover returned to the factory and told her she was pretty enough to model. That was all Norma Jeane needed to hear; in an instant, her old dream of escape had been reactivated.

Conover asked Norma Jeane to pose again. Her husband was due on shore leave just then, so Norma Jeane put the photographer off until Jimmy had gone back to sea. Dougherty left again in June 1945, just as Norma Jeane celebrated her nineteenth birthday. The moment he was gone, she moved out of her in-laws' house, quit her job, and never looked back.

By the end of the month, Conover had taken a set of pictures of Norma Jeane for *Yank* magazine. He showed the photographs to a friend, who in turn put her in touch with the Blue Book Modeling Agency in Los Angeles. The agency passed her on to a film agent, who landed her a screen test at Twentieth Century-Fox. A little over a year after Conover first photographed Norma Jeane, she had divorced her husband, signed a contract at Twentieth, and changed her name to Marilyn Monroe.

Source: *Marilyn Monroe*, by Barbara Leaming, New York: Crown Publishers, 1998

III. COMPREHENSION CHECK

Write answers to the questions.

1. When did Norma Jeane's husband leave for the war?

   _____

2. Where did Norma Jeane go to work?

   _____

3. Who took Norma's picture?

   _____

4. How old was she when she quit her job?

   _____

5. What agency helped her find a film agent?

   _____

6. Which movie company did she screen-test for?

   _____

7. Did she get the job at the movie company?

   _____

IV. VOCABULARY BUILDING

A. Phrasal verbs

Reread the story. Read the definitions on the right, and complete the phrasal verbs.

1. put _____   —postpone
2. look _____   —think about the past
3. ____ turn   —in order; next in a sequence
4. put ____ touch _____ —bring into contact with
5. pass ____   —give something that was received from someone else

B. Use the new words

Complete the sentences with phrasal verbs from Exercise A. Remember to use correct verb form.

1. When he _____ _____ _____ on his childhood, he feels sad.

2. Her mother gave her a ring, which she _____ _____ to her own daughter.

3. The students _____ _____ their homework until the last minute.

4. His professor _____ him _____ _____ _____ a possible job contact.

5. She gave the photos to an agent, who _____ _____ gave them to a film company.

C. Verbs

Read the definitions.

spot	*to see something that you've been looking for or that is difficult to find*
join	*to become a member of a group*
intervene	*to come between in a way that changes the outcome*
pose	*to stand or sit a particular way, usually for a photographer*
land	*to win or get*

D. Use the new words

Complete the sentences with verbs from Exercise C. Remember to use correct verb form.

1. He was very excited when he _____ that high-paying job.

2. The model _____ for photographs all day long.

3. She wanted to work, but her illness _____.

4. They _____ the group of people watching the show.

5. She was happy when she finally_____ her friend in the crowd.

V. UNDERSTANDING GRAMMAR: INFINITIVE OF PURPOSE

A. Read about infinitives of purpose

Infinitives of purpose are used to show a reason for doing something.

> He left his job **to join** the Merchant Marine.
> (He left his job with the purpose of joining the Merchant Marine.)

> The photographers came **to film** women in war work.
> (The photographers came with the intention of filming.)

B. Use infinitives of purpose

Combine the sentences by using an infinitive of purpose.

Example:
> She left home. She wanted to become a movie star.
> *She left home to become a movie star.*

1. He took on an extra job. He wanted to earn more money.

   _____

2. She worked day and night. She wanted to be successful.

   _____

3. She joined an acting class. She wanted to improve her skill.

   _____

4. She put off having children. She wanted to focus on her career.

   _____

5. She acted in commercials and in small TV roles. She wanted to gain experience.

   _____

VI. READ IT AGAIN

Read the paragraphs again. Answer the question.

How did World War II change Norma's life?

_____

_____

ALL THE WORLD'S A STAGE
I. PRE-READING

A. Background information

Before movies and TV shows, people watched plays with live actors for entertainment. And without a doubt, the most famous writer of plays in the English language is William Shakespeare, who died in 1616.

The first two lines of the exerpt in this section are some of Shakespeare's most often–quoted lines.

They come from a speech in his play *As You Like It*. The speaker is comparing life to a play, and he lists seven stages in a man's life. Included below are the first three stages: infant, schoolboy, and lover, and the last one: second childhood.

B. Words to know before you read

Read the words and their definitions.

acts	*the sections of a play*
mewling	*crying*
woeful	*sad*
satchel	*bag*
san	*without*
ballad	*song; often a song that tells a story*

C. Reading strategy

Read the passage. Notice the use of time words to introduce the stages. Write each stage in order.

At first: _____

And then: _____

And then: _____

Last: _____

II. READ

Read the text. Mark the words you don't know, but don't stop reading to look them up.

All the world's a stage,
And all the men and women merely players:
They have their exits and their entrances;
And one man in his time plays many parts,
His acts being seven ages. At first the infant,
Mewling and puking in the nurse's arms.
And then the whining school-boy, with his satchel
And shining morning face, creeping like snail
Unwillingly to school. And then the lover,
Sighing like furnace, with a woeful ballad
Made to his mistress' eyebrow.

Last scene of all,
That ends this strange eventful history,
Is second childishness and mere oblivion,
Sans teeth, sans eyes, sans taste, sans everything.

From *As You Like It* by William Shakespeare.

III. COMPREHENSION CHECK

Circle the letter of the sentence or phrase with the same meaning.

1. *And all the men and women merely players...*

   a. All people are like athletes.

   b. All people are like actors.

2. *And one man in his time plays many parts,*
   His acts being seven ages.

   a. Each man's life is divided into seven stages.

   b. Each man acts like he is seven years old.

3. *And shining morning face...*

   a. The schoolboy's face is oily in the morning.

   b. The schoolboy's face is fresh and clean in the morning.

4. *...creeping like snail*
   Unwillingly to school.

   a. walking slowly and unhappily to school

   b. walking quickly and happily to school

5. *...with a woeful ballad...*

   a. with a sad song

   b. with a long song

6. *...mere oblivion...*

   a. forgetfulness

   b. nothingness

IV. VOCABULARY BUILDING

A. Understanding from context

Read the sentences. Before you look up words in the dictionary, use the context of the sentence to help you match the boldface words with the definitions below.

_____ 1. Why are you angry? I was **merely** trying to help you.

_____ 2. We couldn't see the actors well because we sat very far from the **stage**.

_____ 3. No one could see the thief **creeping** quietly behind the house.

_____ 4. Her eyes were **shining** with happiness.

_____ 5. The little boy was **whining** for candy in the supermarket.

_____ 6. It's cold in here. I think the **furnace** isn't working.

_____ 7. The angry customer was **unwilling** to pay for the dinner.

_____ 8. He was tired after a very **eventful** week.
   a. heater
   b. a raised floor for performances
   c. complaining in a high-pitched, crying voice
   d. only
   e. full of activities
   f. giving out light
   g. moving slowly, close to the ground
   h. not happy to do something

B. Use the new words

Use words from the sentences in Exercise A.

1. The mother was angry at her son because he was
   _____.

2. Make sure the _____ is in good condition to avoid fires.

3. She felt very nervous when she was on the _____ in front of an audience.

4. The newly washed car was _____ in the sun.

5. I'm not the boss; I'm _____ a low-level employee.

6. He didn't see the purpose of the work, so he was _____ to do it.

7. There were several spiders _____ around the wood pile.

8. Her weekend was boring and not very _____.

V. UNDERSTANDING GRAMMAR: *-ING* ADJECTIVES FROM VERBS

A. Read about *-ing* adjectives

In the descriptions *whining school-boy* and *shining morning face*, Shakespeare is using *-ing* adjectives, also known as participial adjectives because they use the form of the present participle of the verb. This kind of adjective usually has the same meaning as the verb it comes from.

> *The boy was crying.*
>   *She gave a tissue to the **crying** boy.*

> *That man ran for two hours.*
>   *The **running** man didn't stop to rest.*

B. Use -ing adjectives

Complete the sentences by using the verb as an adjective.

1. The customers paid for their dinner.

   The manager was pleased to have _____ customers.

2. The boy slept until 7:00 a.m.

   The mother kissed the _____ boy.

3. The birds sing in the trees outside my window.

   I hear _____ birds every morning.

4. The movie captivated her attention.

   She kept her eyes on the _____ movie.

5. She acted on the stage for many years.

   The _____ job didn't pay very well.

VI.   READ IT AGAIN

Read the text again. Answer the question.

Shakespeare's text describes unhappiness at every stage of life. Write the words that describe something negative about each stage.

infant _____

schoolboy _____

lover_____

second childhood _____

6

Eating In, Eating Out

RESTAURANT REVIEWS

I. PRE-READING

A. Background information

These brief restaurant descriptions are from the website videocityguide.com. You can find video reviews of attractions for several cities on the site. The videos that go with these reviews show the restaurant interior and images of the food. These restaurants are in Austin, Texas.

B. Words to know before you read

Match the words to their definitions.

_____ 1. Cajun		a. a person employed to park cars
_____ 2. chic		b. from French-speaking Louisiana
_____ 3. valet		c. restaurant customers
_____ 4. twist		d. places where fish are grown
_____ 5. diners		e. fashionable
_____ 6. fisheries		f. an unexpected development

C. Reading strategy

Quickly read the following restaurant descriptions. Then answer the question.

How many of the descriptions mention steak?

_____

II. READ

Read the text. Mark the words you don't know, but don't stop reading to look them up.

Freda's is a locally owned restaurant specializing in steak and seafood with a Cajun flair. Located near Lakeline Mall, Freda's is upscale yet casual with exceptional food at reasonable prices.

　Carmelo's Italian Restaurant is Austin's answer to an authentic Sicilian kitchen, spiced with continental chic. Carmelo's is located in downtown Austin and offers complimentary valet parking.

Rivals Steakhouse in Downtown Austin offers diners a new twist on the classic steakhouse, featuring the most delicious steaks available in today's market and a stylish comfortable environment.

Welcome to *Truluck's Austin Arboretum*. We are all about fresh seafood, juicy steaks, succulent crab and delicious wines. We are so committed to fresh crab, we have our own fisheries in Naples, Florida. Come enjoy our outdoor patio!

County Line on the Hill has been serving up the biggest, leanest, most awesome barbeque in Texas. Located in the Texas Hill Country we offer outdoor seating with a stellar view!

Source: Austin Restaurants Guide, videocityguide.com

III. COMPREHENSION CHECK

Match the restaurant name to the food it specializes in.

____ 1. Freda's   a. Sicilian food

____ 2. Carmelo's Italian Restaurant   b. fresh crab

____ 3. Rivals Steakhouse   c. barbeque

____ 4. Truluck's Austin Arboretum   d. Cajun food

____ 5. County Line on the Hill   e. steak

IV. VOCABULARY BUILDING

A. Identifying referents

The words below are adjectives. Adjectives describe nouns. Look at the restaurant descriptions, and write the noun (restaurant name) that each adjective describes.

1. upscale   *Freda's* _____

2. casual   _____

3. exceptional   _____

4. authentic   _____

5. continental   _____

6. complimentary   _____

7. stylish   _____

8. juicy   _____

9. succulent   _____

10. lean(est)   _____

11. stellar   _____

B. Identify meaning

Choose the words that have the same meaning as the underlined words.

1. I can't afford to buy a house in that neighborhood. It's a little underlined upscale for me.

   a. crowded

   b. expensive

   c. old

2. I love the casual atmosphere at that coffee shop. You can sit on a sofa, read a book, and drink coffee all day.

   a. relaxed

   b. elegant

   c. exciting

3. This dinner is truly exceptional. I've never tasted anything like it.

   a. large

   b. complicated

   c. unusual

4. The food here is very authentic. It's just like what my mother used to make.

   a. unusual

   b. surprising

   c. real

5. A continental breakfast is usually just bread and coffee. An English breakfast includes eggs and meat.

   a. healthy

   b. European

   c. typical

6. The waiter spilled some water on me. He apologized and brought me a complimentary drink.

   a. delicious

   b. free

   c. sweet

7. That place has old wooden tables and soft chairs. It's not stylish, but it's comfortable.

   a. chic

   b. cheap

   c. interesting

8. This orange is so <u>juicy</u>. I really need a napkin.

   a. heavy

   b. moist

   c. dry

9. Can I have a piece of that <u>succulent</u> orange?

   a. warm and spicy

   b. juicy and delicious

   c. dried-up

10. He's watching his weight, so he always looks for <u>lean</u> beef.

    a. low in fat

    b. high in fat

    c. low-priced

11. All of the food was good, but the fish was just <u>stellar</u>.

    a. expensive

    b. exceptionally good

    c. overcooked

V. UNDERSTANDING GRAMMAR: PARALLEL STRUCTURE

A. Read about parallel structure

When writers link parts of sentences with coordinators like *and*, they use the same parts of speech, and phrases of the same length.

> *Carmelo's <u>is located</u> in downtown Austin and <u>offers</u> valet parking.*
> (present tense verbs)

> *We are all about <u>fresh seafood</u>, <u>juicy steaks</u>, <u>succulent crab</u> and <u>delicious wines</u>.*
> (one adjective + noun)

> *Rivals Steakhouse features <u>the most delicious steaks available in today's market</u> and <u>a stylish comfortable environment</u>.*
> (longer noun phrase)

B. Identify meaning

Complete the sentences with one of the words or phrases from the box.

was terrible	listen to loud music	wave our hands	warm
left	the server didn't take our order	looking	fresh crab

1. I'm never going back to that restaurant. The service was slow and the food
    _____.

2. The soup was cold and the salad was _____ .

3. We had to sit in uncomfortable chairs and _____ .

4. The hostess didn't seat us right away and _____.

5. We had to call out and _____ to get the server's
    attention.

6. She was busy talking to the cook and _____ at a
    magazine.

7. We ordered the large salad, the soup of the day, and
    _____.

8. We _____ early and promised ourselves that we
    wouldn't come back.

VI.   READ IT AGAIN

Read the descriptions again. Answer the question.

In addition to describing the food, each description says something about the
restaurant. Write one thing about each restaurant that is not related to the food.

1. Freda's _____

2. Carmelo's Italian Restaurant _____

3. Rivals Steakhouse _____

4. Truluck's Austin Arboretum _____

5. County Line on the Hill _____

CHOICES ON A DENNY'S® MENU

I.   PRE-READING

A. Background information

The food descriptions below come from a Denny's restaurant menu. There are
Denny's restaurants all over the United States. They have a very large menu and
serve breakfast, lunch, and dinner 24 hours a day.

B. Words to know before you read

*Do you know these food words? Look up any you don't know. Then write each
word in the correct category.*

spinach

caramel

bacon

sausage

prime rib

garlic

pickle

herb

dressing

cucumber

chicken breast

meatball

pasta

mushroom

sauce

toast

shrimp

pot roast

celery

gravy

vegetable (or plant)	meat or seafood	other

C. Reading strategy

Read the name of each of the following dishes. Answer the question.

How many of the items are meat dishes? _____

II. READ

Read the text. Mark the words you don't know, but don't stop reading to look them up.

Breakfast

Veggie-Cheese Omelette
Three-egg omelette with fire-roasted peppers and onions, fresh spinach and mushrooms folded in with diced tomatoes and shredded Cheddar cheese

Banana Caramel French Toast Skillet
Two thick slices of our fabulous French toast topped with fresh banana slices and covered in a sweet caramel sauce. Served with two eggs, two bacon strips or two sausage links.

Lunch

Bowl of Soup
Our soups are kettle-cooked to be rich and hearty. Served with dinner bread. Available from 11 a.m. to 10 p.m.

Prime Rib Philly Melt
Juicy prime rib, mushrooms and onions sautéed, then topped with melted Swiss cheese on grilled ciabatta bread with a zesty garlic spread

Mushroom Swiss Burger
Topped with melted Swiss cheese and mushrooms sautéed in garlic and herbs. Served with lettuce, tomato, pickles and red onions.

Chicken Deluxe Salad
Your choice of golden-fried breaded chicken strips or a grilled seasoned chicken breast sliced on top of crisp mixed greens with grape tomatoes, cucumbers, red onions and Cheddar cheese. Served with the dressing of your choice and dinner bread.

Dinner

Spaghetti and Meatballs
Three seasoned meatballs atop a bed of pasta covered in a rich, meaty tomato sauce. Served with a side of Parmesan cheese and garlic toast.

T-Bone Steak and Shrimp
A tender 13 oz. seasoned T-bone steak with your choice of a grilled shrimp skewer or six golden-fried shrimp. Served with your choice of two sides and dinner bread.

Slow-Cooked Pot Roast
Our slow-cooked pot roast, creamy mashed potatoes and herb-roasted carrots, celery, mushrooms and onions atop grilled ciabatta bread and covered in rich gravy

Source: www.dennys.com

III. COMPREHENSION CHECK

Answer the questions.

1. What vegetables are in the omelette? _____

2. What fruit is on the french toast? _____

3. When can you order the soup? _____

4. What vegetables are with the prime rib? _____

5. What is on top of the hamburger? _____

6. What two kinds of chicken are available for the salad? _____

7. What is on top of the meatballs and pasta? _____

8. What are the shrimp choices with the steak? _____

9. What is on top of the pot roast? _____

IV. VOCABULARY BUILDING

A. Cooking and food preparation

roasted	*slowly cooked in an oven (used for meat and vegetables)*
fire-roasted	*slowly cooked over fire*
kettle-cooked	*cooked in a large, heavy pot*
melted	*changed from solid to liquid with heat*
grilled	*cooked over a fire on a metal grate*
fried	*cooked in oil*
sautéed	*fried quickly in a small amount of butter or oil*
sliced	*cut in thin pieces*

B. Identify the new words

Look back at the menu descriptions. Write the cooking/food preparation method(s) for each food.

1. soup _____

2. peppers _____

3. carrots _____

4. mushrooms _____

5. shrimp _____

6. cheese _____

7. chicken _____

C. Use the new words

Complete the sentences with an appropriate cooking word.

1. He poured a half cup of oil in the pan and then _____ the potatoes.

2. She cleaned the barbecue grate and _____ the sausages.

3. He _____ the butter in the microwave and then poured it over the popcorn.

4. She put a little bit of butter in the pan and quickly _____ the garlic.

5. He put a long fork in the tomato and held it over the fire. He _____ - _____ it until it was black.

V. UNDERSTANDING GRAMMAR: PASSIVE VERBS AND *-ED* ADJECTIVES

A. Read about *-ed* adjectives

Many verbs that can have a passive meaning are also used as adjectives.

> The chicken **was roasted** for two hours. (passive verb)
> We ate **roasted** chicken. (adjective)
> The fish **was fried** in a large pan. (passive verb)
> They served **fried** fish. (adjective)

Notice, however, that some of the *-ed* verbs used in the menu cannot be placed in front of the noun as an adjective:

> fresh spinach and mushrooms <u>folded in</u> with diced tomatoes
> then <u>topped</u> with melted Swiss cheese
> <u>served</u> with lettuce, tomato

We can also say: *The mushrooms were <u>folded in</u> carefully by the cook; The soup was <u>topped</u> with melted Swiss cheese;* or *The burger is <u>served</u> with lettuce and tomato.* These words cannot be used as adjectives before the nouns.

B. Identify the correct form

Complete the sentences with the words from the box. Some of them are adjectives and some of them are verbs.

serve	fried	sauté	roasting
sautéed	frying	serving	roasted

1. Turn on the fan. He's _____ fish again.

2. We usually _____ our hamburgers with french fries.

3. I like to _____ my vegetables in a little bit of butter.

4. They just took that _____ chicken out of the oil.

5. I smell meat _____ in the oven.

6. Are they _____ fish soup today? They don't have it every day.

7. She took a _____ chicken and vegetables out of the oven.

8. Have you tried the _____ spinach? I just used a tiny bit of olive oil.

VI. READ IT AGAIN

Read the menu items again. Answer the questions.

1. How many of the dishes include cheese?

   _____

2. Is the seafood dish under Breakfast, Lunch, or Dinner?

   _____

TRENDS IN SUPERMARKET FOODS

I. PRE-READING

A. Background information

This passage is from the cookbook *Vegetables Every Day* by Jack Bishop. In this section of the introduction, he talks about how cooking and eating have changed in the United States in recent years.

B. Words to know before you read

Match the words to their definitions.

_____ 1. produce aisle	a. one piece of asparagus
_____ 2. transform	b. the ability to get
_____ 3. immigrant	c. the fruit and vegetable section of a market
_____ 4. access	d. a person who comes from foreign country
_____ 5. cuisine	e. change
_____ 6. spear	f. a style of cooking

C. Reading strategy

This passage contains food words that you may not know. These words are not important for understanding the meaning of the passage. Quickly read through the text and draw a line through all of the food words.

II. READ

Read the text. Mark the words you don't know, but don't stop reading to look them up.

The average American supermarket now carries almost 400 kinds of vegetables and fruits during the course of the year. At any given time, most supermarkets have at least 50 vegetables in the produce aisle....

Recent waves of immigration from Asia and Latin America have transformed the produce aisle in most of America. Even though the immigrant population in my area is relatively low, my local supermarket regularly stocks jicama and choyote as well as bok choy and daikon radishes.

In addition to this wide selection of vegetables (the best-ever in history), modern cooks have access to more flavoring ideas and cuisines than ever before. Thirty years ago my mother (as well as most American mothers) prepared asparagus the same way—it was steamed and sauced with butter, lemon or hollandaise. That's how you cooked asparagus.

Today, my mother is just as likely to roast asparagus with rosemary and garlic, Italian style, or dress spears with a Thai peanut sauce. We have the world and its flavors at our fingertips.

Source: *Vegetables Every Day*, by Jack Bishop, New York: HarperCollins, 2001, page xi

III. COMPREHENSION CHECK

Choose the correct answer for each sentence.

1. The main idea of this passage is:
   a. There are many kinds of fruits and vegetables in the world.
   b. The vegetables Americans eat and how they eat them has changed in recent years.
   c. Modern cooks have access to more flavoring ideas and cuisines than ever before.

2. One reason Americans have access to different kinds of vegetables is:
   a. Immigrants have influenced the selection at the grocery store.
   b. Farmers have developed new production methods.
   c. Vegetables are being imported from Latin America.

3. Another way that American habits have changed is:
   a. People are eating a lot less fat and salt.
   b. People are cooking more foods with butter and garlic.
   c. People are using new cooking styles.

IV. VOCABULARY BUILDING

A. Words with multiple meanings

Many words in English have more than one meaning. Sometimes the meanings are related, and sometimes they aren't. Read the following sentences and notice the different meanings of the underlined words.

Same part of speech, related meaning:

1. The supermarkets carry hundreds of fruits and vegetables.

   The students carry books to school.

2. We buy a lot of vegetables over the course of a year.

   The ship took a southern course to avoid the storm.

3. When the economy improved, there was a new wave of immigration.

   There were large waves at the beach today.

   Sound and light travel in waves.

Different part of speech, different (but related) meaning:

4. The asparagus is in the produce aisle.

   Those companies produce a lot of waste.

5. My supermarket stocks some unusual food.

   They lost money on the stocks they bought last year.

Unrelated meanings:

6. She is just as likely to cook Italian style or Thai style.

   I just saw my mother cooking dinner.

B. Use the new words

Use one of the underlined words from Exercise A in each sentence.

1. The groceries were too heavy to _____.

2. Over the _____ of the last four years, I have learned a lot of English.

3. The customers come to the restaurant in _____, at breakfast, lunch, and dinner.

4. No, thank you. I _____ finished eating.

5. Excuse me, do you _____ green tea at this market?

6. What _____ does that ship take to Africa?

7. Sound _____ travel more slowly than light _____.

8. How much oil does that oil well _____?

9. The _____ in that market is always fresh.

10. That store _____ twelve different kinds of milk!

11. The children played in the _____.

12. I worked all day, too. I'm _____ as tired as you are.

13. He put all of his savings into _____.

C. Idioms

at our fingertips = easy to reach

This idiom is often used with *world*, and with information of different kinds.

> He had the world at his fingertips.
> She has the data at her fingertips.

Copy the sentence from the text that uses this idiom.

_____

V. UNDERSTANDING GRAMMAR: *EVEN THOUGH, ALTHOUGH, THOUGH*

A. Read about *even though*

Even though, *although*, and *though* can be used as conjunctions that set up a contrast.

> *Even though* there aren't many immigrants in my neighborhood, my grocery store carries a lot of unusual vegetables.
> *Although* there aren't many immigrants in my neighborhood, my grocery store carries a lot of unusual vegetables.
> *Though* there aren't many immigrants in my neighborhood, my grocery store carries a lot of unusual vegetables.

These three sentences have the same meaning as well as the same grammar. *Even though* emphasizes the contrast. *Though* is less formal and more common than the other two.

If the two clauses are reversed, the meaning of the sentence remains the same, but there is no comma.

> *My grocery store carries a lot of unusual vegetables <u>even though</u> there aren't many immigrants in my neighborhood.*

Unlike the other two, *though* can be used as an adverb at the end of the sentence.

> *That was a delicious meal!*
> *It was expensive, **though**.*

B. Use the grammar

Combine the sentences using though/although/even though. *Don't change the order of the sentences. Make sure you put the conjunction in front of the correct clause, and use a comma if necessary.*

1. I didn't have much money. I bought an expensive dinner.

   _____

2. I buy that vegetable because it's healthy. I don't really like it.

   _____

3. I don't usually like cabbage. I love bok choy.

   _____

4. The market carries a lot of Latin American produce. They don't stock jicama.

   _____

5. We don't have access to a wide variety of fruits. It is possible to find unusual vegetables.

   _____

VI.   READ IT AGAIN

Read the passage again. Answer the question.

The writer is talking about international influence on American eating habits. What specific regions does he mention?

_____

HUNTING FOR DINNER

I.   PRE-READING

A. Background information

This passage is from the book *The Omnivore's Dilemma* by Michael Pollan. An omnivore is an animal that eats both plants and animals. Pollan writes about the food system in the United States. He describes large-scale farming and ranching and compares them to more traditional small-scale food production. He talks about the health effects, the economic effects, and the ethical aspects of modern food production. In one section of the book, Pollan describes his effort to eat a meal that only includes food that he has planted, gathered, or hunted himself. The passage below comes from the chapter where he hunts and kills an animal for the first time in his life.

B. Words to know before you read

These words are all related to guns. Match them to their definitions.

____ 1. cocked   a. the tube-shaped part of the gun

____ 2. safety   b. the part you pull to fire the gun

____ 3. barrel   c. a device on a gun that you look
                                       through

____ 4. trigger   d. ready for shooting

____ 5. sight   e. the part of the gun that prevents
                                       accidental firing

C. Reading strategy

The italicized text in this reading indicates people talking (direct speech). Look quickly through the passage, and find all of the sentences with italicized words. Answer the question.

What is the name of the man who is teaching Pollan how to hunt?

_____

II. READ

Read the text. Mark the words you don't know, but don't stop reading to look them up.

I touched Angelo on the shoulder and pointed toward the pigs. *What should I do?* This time my gun was cocked, of course, and now, for the first time, I took off the safety. *Should I shoot? No, you wait,* Angelo said. *See—they're coming down the hill now.* I followed the pigs with the barrel of my gun, trying to get one of them in my sight. My finger rested lightly on the trigger, and it took all the self-restraint I could summon not to squeeze, but I didn't have a clear shot—too many trees stood in the way. *Take your time,* Angelo whispered. They will come to us. And so they did, following the streambed down to the road directly in front of us, moving toward us in an excruciatingly slow parade. I have no idea how long it took the pigs to pick their way down the steep hill, whether it was minutes or just seconds. At last the first animal, a big black one, stepped out into the clearing of the dirt road, followed by another that was just as big but much lighter in color. The second pig presented its flank. *Now!* Angelo whispered. *This is your shot!*

Source: *The Omnivore's Dilemma,* by Michael Pollan, New York: Penguin Books, 2006, p. 351

III. COMPREHENSION CHECK

Mark the sentences T (True) or F (False).

_____ 1. They are hunting pigs.

_____ 2. Pollan shoots a pig right away.

_____ 3. There were a lot of trees in the area.

_____ 4. The pigs were walking on flat ground.

_____ 5. Angelo told Pollan to shoot the black pig.

IV. VOCABULARY BUILDING

A. Understanding from context

Read the words and definitions. Then write each word in one of the following sentences.

self-restraint	*self-control*
summon	*call urgently*
excruciating	*painful*
steep	*sharply rising, vertical*
parade	*a formal walk or march*
squeeze	*press together, usually with the fingers*
clearing	*an opening in the trees*
flank	*the side of an animal's body*

1. The penguins moved through the snow in one long
   _____.

2. It was dark under the trees but sunny in the
   _____.

3. We were not happy about walking up the _____
   mountain.

4. Walking up the mountain was _____.

5. They _____ the fruit until the juice comes out.

6. The child was nervous when he heard his mother _____ him from the
   house.

7. The horse had a large black spot on its _____.

8. Adults have more _____ than children do.

V. UNDERSTANDING GRAMMAR: *-ING* PHRASES

A. Read about *-ing* phrases

The *-ing* form (also called the present participle) is sometimes used to combine ideas. The sentence:

I followed the pigs with the barrel of my gun, trying to get one of them in my sight.

can be rewritten as two sentences:

I followed the pigs with the barrel of my gun. I tried to get one of them in my sight.

The writer's version is better because it avoids repeating the subject, and the two actions fit closely together.

Note: When using participial phrases, writers must be careful that the subject of the participle is the subject of the sentence. A sentence like this: *I followed the pigs with the barrel of my gun, picking their way down the hill* is INCORRECT because *followed* and *picking* have different subjects.

B. Identify participial phrases

Read the sentences. Underline the -ing form and its subject in each sentence.

1. They cooked all evening, roasting potatoes, beef, and vegetables.

2. She climbed the steep mountain, breathing hard and sweating.

3. He wrote about the modern food system, describing in detail the operations of a large farm.

C. Use the grammar

Combine the sentences using a participial phrase.

1. We bought the dinner. We paid for the meal, the drinks, and the tip.

    _____

2. She worked on a modern small-scale farm. She raised chickens and grew organic vegetables.

    _____

3. She took care of the chickens. She allowed them to wander free and eat insects.

    _____

4. They walked through the forest. They moved slowly as they listened for the sounds of the animals.

    _____

VI. READ IT AGAIN

Read the passage again. Answer the question.

The writer is nervous and excited on his first hunt. What words in the passage give you a clue about how he feels?

_____

CHRISTMAS MORNING BREAKFAST

I. PRE-READING

A. Background information

This passage comes from *Little Women* by Louisa May Alcott. This story about four sisters was published in 1880, but it has remained popular throughout the years. In this chapter, the girls have opened their Christmas presents and have been waiting for their mother, Mrs. March, to come home before they start breakfast.

B. Words to know before you read

Match the words to their definitions.

_____ 1. huddle	a. place one thing on top of another
_____ 2. suffer	b. quickly, without thought
_____ 3. exclaim	c. thing
_____ 4. impetuously	d. crowd together
_____ 5. article	e. brave
_____ 6. pile	f. say enthusiastically
_____ 7. heroic	g. experience something bad

C. Reading strategy

Quickly scan the following text for names. Write the names of the four sisters.

_____

_____

_____

_____

II. READ

Read the text. Mark the words you don't know, but don't stop reading to look them up.

"Merry Christmas, little daughters! I'm glad you began at once, and hope you will keep on. But I want to say one word before we sit down. Not far away from here lies a poor woman with a little newborn baby. Six children are huddled into one bed to keep from freezing, for they have no fire. There is nothing to eat over there, and the oldest boy came to tell they were suffering hunger and cold. My girls, will you give them your breakfast as a Christmas present?"

They were all unusually hungry, having waited nearly an hour, and for a minute no one spoke, only a minute, for Jo exclaimed impetuously—

"I'm so glad you came before we began!"

"May I go and help carry the things to the poor little children?" asked Beth eagerly.

"I shall take the cream and the muffins," added Amy, heroically giving up the article she most liked.

Meg was already covering the buckwheats, and piling the bread into one big plate.

"I thought you'd do it," said Mrs. March, smiling as if satisfied. "You shall all go and help me, and when we come back we will have bread and milk for breakfast, and make it up at dinnertime."

Source: *Little Women*, by Louisa May Alcott

III. COMPREHENSION CHECK

Mark the sentences T (True) or F (False).

_____ 1. When Mrs. March comes in, the girls are sitting at the table.

_____ 2. The poor woman has five children.

_____ 3. Mrs. March learned about the family's problem from the oldest son.

_____ 4. The sisters are not hungry.

_____ 5. Beth really wants to help take the food to the poor family.

_____ 6. Amy's favorite breakfast food is cream and muffins.

_____ 7. Jo gets the food ready to take to the family.

_____ 8. The sisters will have bread and milk for dinner.

IV. VOCABULARY BUILDING

A. Adjectives and adverbs

Read the words in the chart. Write the correct form for each word to complete the following sentences.

adjective	adverb
heroic	heroically
eager	eagerly
impetuous	impetuously

1. The soldier _____ gave his life for his country.

2. The children were _____ to help their mother.

3. He doesn't think before he acts—he's very _____.

4. She acted _____, and then she was sorry.

5. When they asked for help, the young women responded
    _____.

6. The soldier earned a medal for his _____
    actions.

B. Verbs

The verbs in the chart are in base form. Write them in the correct form in the following sentences.

exclaim	pile	huddle
make up	keep on	suffer

1. You will have to _____ the test you missed.

2. "It's beautiful!" she _____ happily.

3. The children _____ together to protect their
    little sister.

4. I called him, but he _____ working. He didn't
    hear me.

5. Please help those poor people. They are _____.

6. She _____ up the coins in a tall stack.

V. UNDERSTANDING GRAMMAR: REQUESTS WITH *MAY, CAN*, AND *COULD*

A. Read about *may, can*, and *could*

In the reading passage, Beth asks for permission to go with her mother with the question: *May I go. . .?* To the modern reader, this sounds old-fashioned because *May I* questions have become very formal—most people don't use them within the family anymore. There are, however, situations where questions with *May I* are very appropriate:

- A clerk in a store asks, *May I help you?*
- When you ask a favor of a stranger you can use *May I*; for example, *Excuse me. May I take this chair?*
- At someone's home, you can ask, *May I use your restroom?*

All of these questions can also be asked with *can* or *could*, but *may* is much more formal.

Note: *May* requests are only used with the subject *I*. When the subject is *you*, you must use *can* or *could*.

> Excuse me. **Could you** help me with this? **Can you** pass the butter?

Can is less formal than *could*.

B. Identify forms

Complete the conversations with can, could, *or* may.

1. Brother: Hey, _____ you bring me a soda?
   Sister: Sure.

2. Clerk: _____ I help you with something?
   Customer: No, thanks. I'm just looking.

3. Coworker: _____ you please make this copy for me? I have to leave.
   Coworker: No problem.

4. Friend: _____ you hand me the remote?
   Friend: Uh-huh.

5. Employee: Excuse me, Mr. Silva. _____ I talk to you for a minute?
   Mr. Silva: Of course.

VI.   READ IT AGAIN

Read the passage again. Answer the question.

Why is Mrs. March satisfied?

_____

Playing the Game

THE RULES FOR CHECKERS

I. PRE-READING

A. Background information

Checkers is one of the oldest known board games. Many people believe that it is related to a game played in Ancient Egypt, and versions of it have been popular around the world for centuries. The rules and number of pieces may vary in different countries, but it is basically the same game everywhere. In most English-speaking countries it is called Draughts (pronounced "drafts"). It is only called checkers in North America. The following U.S. rules are from Eric Arneson on the website About.com.

B. Words to know before you read

Match the words to their definitions.

_____ 1. alternate		a. jump
_____ 2. diagonal		b. a flat round object
_____ 3. disc		c. an opportunity to play
_____ 4. opponent		d. take turns
_____ 5. capture		e. the person someone is competing against in a game
_____ 6. turn		f. catch, take control of
_____ 7. leap		g. from an opposite corner

C. Reading strategy

Quickly scan parts 1, 2, and 3 of the following text for numbers. Then answer the questions.

1. How many colored discs does each player start with?

_____

2. How many squares are on the board?

_____

II. READ

Read the text. Mark the words you don't know, but don't stop reading to look them up.

1. Checkers is played by two players. Each player begins the game with 12 colored discs. (Typically, one set of pieces is black and the other red.)

2. The board consists of 64 squares, alternating between 32 dark and 32 light squares. It is positioned so that each player has a light square on the right side corner closest to him or her.

3. Each player places his or her pieces on the 12 dark squares closest to him or her.

4. Black moves first. Players then alternate moves.

5. Moves are allowed only on the dark squares, so pieces always move diagonally. Single pieces are always limited to forward moves (toward the opponent).

6. A piece making a non-capturing move (not involving a jump) may move only one square.

7. A piece making a capturing move (a jump) leaps over one of the opponent's pieces, landing in a straight diagonal line on the other side. Only one piece may be captured in a single jump; however, multiple jumps are allowed on a single turn.

8. When a piece is captured, it is removed from the board.

9. If a player is able to make a capture, there is no option—the jump must be made. If more than one capture is available, the player is free to choose whichever he or she prefers.

10. When a piece reaches the farthest row from the player who controls that piece, it is crowned and becomes a king. One of the pieces that had been captured is placed on top of the king so that it is twice as high as a single piece.

11. Kings are limited to moving diagonally, but may move both forward and backward. (Remember that single pieces, i.e., non-kings, are always limited to forward moves.)

12. Kings may combine jumps in several directions—forward and backward— on the same turn. Single pieces may shift direction diagonally during a multiple capture turn, but must always jump forward (toward the opponent).

13. A player wins the game when the opponent cannot make a move. In most cases, this is because all of the opponent's pieces have been captured, but it could also be because all of his pieces are blocked in.

Source: boardgames.about.com/cs/checkersdraughts/ht/play_checkers.htm

III. COMPREHENSION CHECK

Mark the sentences T (True) or F (False).

_____ 1. Checkers is a game for four players.

_____ 2. The player using the black pieces moves first.

_____ 3. Pieces can be moved to dark or light squares.

_____ 4. A player can capture multiple pieces in a single jump.

IV. VOCABULARY BUILDING

A. Word families

Read the word families in the chart. Then choose the correct form for each sentence.

verb	adjective	adverb
alternate	alternating	
diagonal	diagonally	
typical	typically	
oppose	opposing	
shift	shifting	

1. The governor made negative statements about his ___ during the election.

   a. opponent

   b. oppose

2. An ___ current is one that sometimes reverses directions.

   a. alternate

   b. alternating

3. She ___ her position to make room on the bench.

   a. shifting

   b. shifted

4. The teachers ___ any changes to the school rules.

   a. opposing

   b. opposed

5. A red circle with a ___ line across it means "no."

   a. diagonal

   b. diagonally

6. On a ___ day, I wake up at 6:00.

   a. typical

   b. typically

7. For sore muscles, ___ between heat and cold.

   a. alternating

   b. alternate

8. Some countries have crosswalks that run ___ through the intersection.

   a. diagonal

   b. diagonally

9. We sometimes refer to things that constantly change as "___ sands."

   a. shifting

   b. shift

10. I'm surprised Mark isn't here. He ___ arrives by 9:00.

    a. typical

    b. typically

11. The home team wore white uniforms and the ___ team wore blue.

    a. opponent

    b. opposing

B. Use the new words

Complete the sentences with words from the chart in Exercise A. Use appropriate forms.

1. He drew a line _____ across the paper.

2. The _____ team was fast and strong.

3. She _____ stays late at work, but today she left early.

4. My husband likes the Chinese restaurant and I like the Italian one, so we _____ between them.

5. He just looked like a _____ teenager. I don't remember anything unusual about him.

6. The coach made the players run _____ across the field for practice.

7. Try to learn as much as you can about your _____ before you play against him or her.

8. She wore striped pajamas, in _____ blues and yellows.

9. Businesses have to keep up with the _____ tastes of consumers.

10. No one _____ the mayor in the last election. He won easily.

11. The box fell over when the items inside it _____.

V. UNDERSTANDING GRAMMAR: *SO* VS. *SO THAT*

A. Read about *so* and *so that*

So is a coordinating conjunction. It combines two independent clauses. The second clause is a **result** of the first. The two clauses are separated with a comma.

> *We needed bread, **so I went to the store.***
> *They were hungry, **so they ate dinner.***

So that is a subordinating conjunction. It combines a dependent clause with an independent clause. Unlike other subordinating conjunctions, however, we rarely use so that at the beginning of a sentence. *So that* introduces a purpose (not a result). We often use so that with a modal. like *can* or *could*.

> *He saved money **so that he could buy a house.***
> *Please close the door so **that we can have some privacy.***

In speaking and informal writing, we often use *so* to mean *so that*. You can tell the difference between them because of the meaning. In writing, you can also tell the difference because we use a comma before the coordinating conjunction *so*, but not before *so that* (even when it's shortened to *so*).

B. Identify forms

Complete the sentences with comma + so or with so that. Do not shorten so that to so.

1. Martina didn't study _____ she failed the test.

2. Teresa woke up early _____ she could get to work on time.

3. The students didn't sleep last night _____ they are very tired today.

4. Alan doesn't understand the lectures _____ he's not very interested in the class.

5. I'll call you tonight _____ we can make plans for the weekend.

6. Our favorite restaurant was closed _____ we went to a different one.

7. They closed the windows _____ the neighbors wouldn't hear the piano.

8. I washed dishes last night _____ it's your turn tonight.

VI. READ IT AGAIN

Read the rules for playing checkers again. Answer the question.

Why would a player want to reach the farthest edge of the board as soon as possible?

_____

"TAKE ME OUT TO THE BALL GAME"

I. PRE-READING

<u>A.</u> Background information

A baseball game is divided into nine *innings*, during which the teams take turns playing offense and defense. When people go to baseball games in the United States and Canada, it is traditional to stand up in the middle of the seventh inning when the teams trade places on the field. This is called "the seven inning stretch." Nowadays, most baseball stadiums play "Take Me Out to the Ball Game" during the seventh inning stretch. The audience sings along, often changing the words "home team" to the name of the local team. The song was written in 1908 by Jack Norworth and was first sung at a major league baseball game in the 1930s. Only the chorus is sung at the games.

<u>B.</u> Words to know before you read

Match the words to their definitions.

_____ 1. mad

_____ 2. root for

_____ 3. Cracker Jack

_____ 4. sou

_____ 5. beau

_____ 6. crew

a. an old-fashioned word for "boyfriend"

b. old-fashioned French coin, used like "penny"

c. crazy

d. team

e. cheer for

f. a snack with popcorn and peanuts that first appeared in 1896 and has a strong association with baseball

Baseball words:

_____ 1. strike

_____ 2. umpire

a. a baseball game official

b. a missed hit; a player with three strikes is "out." After three outs, the offense and defense team switch places.

<u>C.</u> Reading strategy

Read the song quickly and without stopping. Then answer the question.

What did Katie Casey love?

_____

II. READ

Read the text. Mark the words you don't know, but don't stop reading to look them up.

1908 Version

Katie Casey was baseball mad,
Had the fever and had it bad.
Just to root for the home town crew,
Ev'ry sou
Katie blew.
On a Saturday her young beau
Called to see if she'd like to go
To see a show, but Miss Kate said "No,
I'll tell you what you can do:"

Chorus:

Take me out to the ball game,
Take me out with the crowd;
Buy me some peanuts and Cracker Jack,
I don't care if I never get back.
Let me root, root, root for the home team,
If they don't win, it's a shame.
For it's one, two, three strikes, you're out,
At the old ball game.

Katie Casey saw all the games,
Knew the players by their first names.
Told the umpire he was wrong,
All along,
Good and strong.
When the score was just two to two,
Katie Casey knew what to do,
Just to cheer up the boys she knew,
She made the gang sing this song:

[repeat chorus]

III. COMPREHENSION CHECK

Mark the sentences T (True) or F (False).

_____ 1. Katie wanted to go to a show with her boyfriend.

_____ 2. She wanted to cheer for her home team.

_____ 3. She went to a lot of baseball games.

_____ 4. She disagreed with the umpire.

_____ 5. She wanted to go home early.

IV. VOCABULARY BUILDING

A. Understanding from context

Read the phrases. Before you look up words in the dictionary, use the context of the sentence to help you match the boldface words with the following definitions.

_____ 1. He **blew** all of his money on a vacation, and now he can't pay his bills.

_____ 2. Our team started winning, so suddenly everyone has baseball **fever**.

_____ 3. We're leaving in the morning, but I think we'll **get back** before 5:00.

_____ 4. We won! The final **score** was 5 to 3.

_____ 5. Alice baked a cake to **cheer up** her sad friend.

_____ 6. I feel like having a party. Let's call up the **gang**.
   a. to make happier
   b. to return
   c. love of something, especially a sport or something that is very popular at the moment
   d. the points in a game
   e. a group of friends (informal). This word often means a group of criminals, but not always.
   f. spend, usually unwisely

B. Use the new words

Fill in the blanks with the words from Exercise A. Use correct verb forms.

1. Every four years, everyone around here gets Olympic _____.

2. I need to _____ my brother. His team lost the game and he's very upset.

3. There's a big _____ of teenagers that hangs out in the park every evening.

4. What time will you _____ from work tonight?

5. Don't _____ your money on a new bike. I'll give you my extra one.

6. I missed the end of the game. What was the final _____?

V. UNDERSTANDING GRAMMAR: DIRECT SPEECH VS. REPORTED SPEECH

A. Read about direct and reported speech

Writers have two ways of describing what people say. With "direct speech," they report someone's exact words. Direct speech has quotation marks and is often introduced with words like *say* or *ask* (called "reporting verbs").

   She *said*, *"I'll call you when I get back."*

Often, however, we do not quote the exact words that people say, but instead use "reported speech." In reported speech, verb tenses change to go along with the reporting verb. Here are some examples of these changes:

Direct Speech		Reported Speech
He said, "I love baseball."	→	He said he* loved baseball.
She said, "I went to the game."	→	She said she* had gone to the game.
Tom said, "You are going to lose."	→	Tom told us** we were going to lose.
Mona said, "You'll enjoy the show."	→	Mona said that*** I would enjoy the show.

*Notice that pronouns also change when we move from direct to reported speech.
**We usually use "tell" with reported speech, not direct speech. It is followed by an indirect object (e.g., *me, us, him, them*).
***We sometimes use *that* after *say* or after *tell* + indirect object.

B. Identify reported speech

Read the sentences. Match the direct speech to the reported speech.

____ 1. He said, "You won't win." a. He said we were going to win.

____ 2. He said, "You won." b. He said we won.

____ 3. He said, "You're going to win." c. He said we couldn't win.

____ 4. He said, "You win." d. He said we wouldn't win.

____ 5. He said, "You can't win." e. He said we hadn't won.

____ 6. He said, "You haven't won." f. He said we had won.

C. Identify direct and reported speech

Read the sentences. Circle the matching sentence.

1. Tony said, "The gang is coming over at 4:00."

   a. Tony said the gang came over at 4:00.

   b. Tony said the gang was coming over at 4:00.

2. Kim said she had blown her whole paycheck on a pair of shoes.

   a. Kim said, "I blow my whole paycheck on a pair of shoes."

   b. Kim said, "I blew my whole paycheck on a pair of shoes."

3. The manager said he would fix the photocopier.

    a. The manager said, "I fixed the photocopier."

    b. The manager said, "I'll fix the photocopier."

4. Jordi said, "I'm going to drive you home."

    a. Jordi said that he was going to drive me home.

    b. Jordi said that he had driven me home.

5. Alice told me that she was quitting.

    a. Alice said, "I quit."

    b. Alice said, "I'm quitting."

VI. READ IT AGAIN

Read the song again. Find one example of direct speech and one example of reported speech.

_____

_____

THE ATTRACTION OF GOLF

I. PRE-READING

A. Background information

Tiger Woods is an American golfer who was one of the most successful and well paid athletes in the world during the late 1990s and early 2000s. He holds many golfing records and made millions of dollars advertising products. In 2009 he took a leave of absence from golf because of a scandal. He has since returned to golf but has not achieved his former level of success. The following passage is from his autobiography, *How I Play Golf*, which came out in 2001 when he was at the height of his fame.

B. Words to know before you read

Match the words to their definitions.

_____ 1. be infatuated with	a. using your own power or resources
_____ 2. club	b. surrender; give in
_____ 3. toddler	c. a phrase that people say too often
_____ 4. self-reliance	d. in the end
_____ 5. succumb	e. the "stick" used for hitting a golf ball
_____ 6. cliché	f. love intensely
_____ 7. ultimately	g. a small child (1–2 years old)

C. Reading strategy

Quickly read the paragraph looking for two names. Then answer the questions.

1. Which two people does he name?

   _____

2. Who are they?

   _____

II. READ

Read the text. Mark the words you don't know, but don't stop reading to look them up.

I have been infatuated with the game since my pop first put a club in my hands when I was a toddler. I was an only child, and the club and ball became my playmates. That feeling of solitude and self-reliance enhanced the game's attraction for me and endures today. I suspect that is true of most people who have succumbed to the lure of the game. I recall from conversations with two of the greatest golfers of our time—Arnold Palmer and Jack Nicklaus—that the game had a similar appeal for them. Golf affords you supreme independence. The cliché about the game being you against the golf course is only partly true. Ultimately, it is you against yourself. It always comes down to how well you know yourself, your ability to execute under pressure that is mostly self-created. Ultimately, you must have the heart and head to play a shot and the courage to accept the consequences.

Source: *How I Play Golf*, by Tiger Woods, New York: Warner Books, 2001, p. 2

III. COMPREHENSION CHECK

Mark the sentences T (True) or F (False).

_____ 1. Tiger started playing golf when he was very young.

_____ 2. He had brothers and sisters.

_____ 3. He believes that golf encourages players to be very independent.

IV. VOCABULARY BUILDING

A. Understanding from context

Read the words and definitions. Find the word in the passage and choose the definition that fits best. (Both are possible definitions of the word.)

_____ 1. solitude
     a. a lonely place
     b. the state of being alone

_____ 2. appeal*
   a. the quality of being attractive
   b. a legal request

_____ 3. lure*
   a. a type of bait used in fishing
   b. a very attractive quality

_____ 4. endure
   a. continue
   b. suffer

_____ 5. enhance
   a. improve
   b. make stronger

_____ 6. afford
   a. give an opportunity for
   b. have enough money for

_____ 7. execute
   a. perform an action
   b. kill someone

*The meaning of these two words is very similar, but they are used differently. *Lure* is stronger, it cannot be used with quantifiers like "a lot" and "much," and we almost always use it in the phrase "the lure of the ___" (*the lure of the city, the lure of easy money*).

Appeal is not as strong as *lure* and it can be used with quantifiers. We can use it like *lure* (*the appeal of the city*), but it can also be used in other ways, especially after the verb *have* (*That style has a lot of appeal for me*).

B. Use the new words

Complete each sentence with one of the words from Exercise A.

1. When I travel, reading about local history really _____ my appreciation of the places I visit.

2. No one is home today, and I'm enjoying my _____.

3. The house was very well built and has _____ for many years.

4. My new job _____ the opportunity to use the skills I've learned.

5. Everyone loves that restaurant, but it doesn't have much _____ for me.

6. It's always amazing to watch an Olympic skater _____ a perfect jump.

7. He didn't really want the job, but he couldn't resist the _____ of a big paycheck.

V. UNDERSTANDING GRAMMAR: COMPLEX SUBJECTS

A. Read about complex subjects

{T}Writers form complex subjects in a variety ways. One of them is to use a prepositional phrase within the subject. Look at this sentence from the reading. The subject is underlined, the prepositional phrase is bracketed, and the verb is circled:

> The cliché [about the game being you against the golf course](is)only partly true.

This one has two verbs:

> That feeling [of solitude and self-reliance] (enhanced) the game's attraction for me and (endures) today.

B. Identify forms

Read the sentences. Underline the subject. Bracket the prepositional phrase. Circle the verb or verbs.

1. The top athletes in major sports make a lot of money.

2. The book about his experiences growing up was very interesting.

3. Driving under the influence of alcohol is a serious offense.

4. Several of the restaurants around town are offering special discounts this week.

5. The lines on his forehead deepened as he got older.

6. The witness's explanation of the events didn't make any sense.

VI. READ IT AGAIN

Read the excerpt again. Answer the question.

Why does Tiger Woods love golf?

THE INVENTION OF BASKETBALL

I. PRE-READING

A. Background information

Most sports have ancient origins, but basketball is unusual because we know exactly when and where it was invented. In 1891, Dr. James Naismith wanted to invent a game to improve the physical fitness of young athletes during the cold Massachusetts winters. The young men were not very interested in playing games in the gym, and Dr. Naismith tried a number of experiments. He wanted something that would give the men plenty of exercise but would also be fun. In this passage from his book *Basketball: Its Origin and Development*, he describes the first time he tried the new game.

B. Words to know before you read

Match the words to their definitions.

_____ 1. thumbtack

_____ 2. bulletin board

_____ 3. tackle

_____ 4. ringleader

_____ 5. surmise

_____ 6. death knell

_____ 7. roll

a. a person who leads a group of people who are doing something wrong

b. guess

c. the sound of a bell to mark someone's death

d. a board for displaying notices

e. a list of students' names

f. a short pin with a flat top

g. a position in American football; the knocking down of another player

C. Reading strategy

Quickly read the first paragraph looking for the name Frank Mahan. Answer the question.

Who was Frank Mahan?

_____

II. READ

Read the text. Mark the words you don't know, but don't stop reading to look them up.

When Miss Lyons finished typing the rules, it was almost class time, and I was anxious to get down to the gym. I took the rules and made my way down the stairs. Just inside the door there was a bulletin board for notices. With thumb tacks I fastened the rules to this board and then walked across the gym. I was sure in my own mind that the game was good, but it needed a real test. I felt that its success or failure depended largely on the way that the class received it. The first member of the class to arrive was Frank Mahan. He was a southerner from North Carolina, had played tackle on the football team, and was the ringleader of the group. He saw me standing with a ball in my hand, and perhaps surmised that another experiment was to be tried. He looked up at the basket on one end of the gallery, and then his eyes turned to me. He gazed at me for an instant, and then looked toward the other end of the gym. Perhaps I was nervous, because his exclamation sounded like a death knell as he said, "Huh! another new game!"

When the class arrived, I called the roll and told them that I had another game, which I felt sure would be good. I promised them that if this was a failure, I would not try any more experiments. I then read the rules from the bulletin board and proceeded to organize the game. There were eighteen men in the class; I selected two captains and had them choose sides. When the teams were chosen, I placed the men on the floor. There were three forwards, three centers, and three backs on each team. I chose two of the center men to jump, then threw the ball between them. It was the start of the first basketball game and the finish of the trouble with that class.

Source: *Basketball: Its Origin and Development*, by James Naismith, Kindle edition, Kindle locations 483–87

III. COMPREHENSION CHECK

Write answers to the questions.

1. What did he do with the rules?

    _____

2. How did he feel about the game?

    _____

3. Why did Frank Mahan's comment sound like a death knell to him?

    _____

4. What did he promise the class?

    _____

5. Was the game a success that day?

    _____

IV. VOCABULARY BUILDING

A. Understanding from context

Find these words in the reading. Then match each with the correct definition.

_____ 1. failure   a. attached

_____ 2. made my way   b. a moment

_____ 3. fastened   c. looked at

_____ 4. gazed   d. begin and complete an action

_____ 5. instant   e. opposite of success

_____ 6. proceeded to   f. moved forward

B. Use the new words

Fill in each blank using one of the words from Exercise A.

1. The bird landed on the branch for an _____. Then it flew away.

2. The old lady slowly _____ down the stairs.

3. The deer _____ at me for a moment before it ran away.

4. I wanted to leave, but he _____ tell me a long story, and I had to wait for him to finish.

5. We were very unhappy about the _____ of our experiment.

6. She _____ several flowers to her hat for the costume.

V. UNDERSTANDING GRAMMAR: CONNECTING SENTENCES WITH *THEN* AND *AND THEN*

A. Read about *then*

Then is a very common connecting word, often used to clarify a time sequence. It tells us that something happened next.
    And then can be used to connect two verbs with the same subject.

> *With thumb tacks I **fastened** the rules to this board and then **walked** across the gym.*

In this kind of sentence, it's possible to remove *and* for stylistic effect.

> *I **chose** two of the center men to jump, then **threw** the ball between them.*

And then can also be used to connect two clauses. It is not possible to remove *and* in this kind of sentence.

> *He looked up at the basket on one end of the gallery, **and then** his eyes turned to me.*

Another way to write this would be:

> *He looked up at the basket on one end of the gallery. **Then** his eyes turned to me.*

Notice that *then* is not a coordinating conjunction. If we are connecting clauses, we must use *and then*.
    Another common placement for *then* is between the subject and verb.

> *I then **read** the rules from the bulletin board and proceeded to organize the game.*

B. Identify forms

Complete the sentences with then *or* and then. *(In some cases, both are possible.)*

1. The player stole the ball _____ ran down the court.

2. We arrived at 4:00. _____ we stood in line for two hours.

3. He stormed into the room _____ proceeded to shout at the employees.

4. Marcia looked everywhere for her keys. She _____ realized that she had left them in the car the night before.

5. He grew a beard _____ changed his hair style. I hardly recognize him anymore.

VI.   READ IT AGAIN

Read the passage again. Answer the question.

Why was the basketball game the end of the trouble with the class?

_____

TOWARD THE FINISHING LINE
I.   PRE-READING

A. Background information

Dick Francis was a jockey (a racehorse rider) until he was 37 years old. He retired because of multiple injuries, and as soon as he quit racing, he wrote his first book, an autobiography. Then he began writing mystery novels set in the horse-racing world. He went on to write 40 international bestsellers. His books are full of detailed descriptions of the horse-racing world. The following passage is from *Break In*, which was published in 1986. Dick Francis died in 2010.

B. Words to know before you read

Match the words to their definitions.

_____ 1. roar   a. a group

_____ 2. willfully   b. long, loud sound

_____ 3. stride   c. go quickly past

_____ 4. sweep past   d. with determination

_____ 5. bunch   e. pace or step

Horse-racing words:

___ 1. gallop

    a. a long, narrow strap used to control a horse

___ 2. reins

    b. the person who rides a horse in a race

___ 3. jockey

    c. the fastest pace of a horse

C. Reading strategy

Quickly read the paragraph. Then answer the questions.

1. What is the name of the horse?

    _____

2. Did he win the race?

    _____

II. READ

Read the text. Mark the words you don't know, but don't stop reading to look them up.

I could dimly hear the crowd roaring, which one usually couldn't. North Face put his ears back and galloped with a flat, intense, bloody-minded stride, accelerating toward the place he knew was his, that he'd so willfully rejected, that he wanted in his heart.

I flattened myself forward to the line of his neck to cut the wind resistance: kept the reins tight, my body still, my weight steady over his shoulders, all the urging a matter of mind and hands, a matter of giving that fantastic racing creature his maximum chance.

The others were tiring, the incline slowing them drastically as it did always to so many. North Face swept past a bunch of them as they wavered and there was suddenly only one in front, one jockey who thought he was surely winning and had half dropped his hands.

One could feel sorry for him, but he was a gift from heaven. North Face caught him at a rush a bare stride from the winning post, and I knew for a certainty at once that we had won.

Source: *Break In*, by Dick Francis, New York: Berkley Publishing Group, 1986, p. 6

III. COMPREHENSION CHECK

Mark the sentences T (True) or F (False).

___ 1. There were a lot of people watching the race.

___ 2. North Face was a good racehorse.

___ 3. North Face was in front from the beginning of the race.

IV. VOCABULARY BUILDING

A. Understanding from context

Read the sentences. Before you look up words in the dictionary, use the context of the sentence to help you match the boldface words with the following definitions.

_____ 1. I was **dimly** aware of the noise in the kitchen while I was sleeping.

_____ 2. The car should have stopped. Instead, it **accelerated** through the intersection.

_____ 3. Mark **rejected** the job offer. He thinks he can find something better.

_____ 4. The new boss wanted to make changes, but she met a lot of **resistance** from employees who liked things the way they were.

_____ 5. After the hurricane damage, the government **urged** residents to prepare for the next emergency.

_____ 6. I'm okay walking on flat ground, but when we get to an **incline**, I start having trouble.

_____ 7. The department needs to **drastically** cut spending or the company will go out of business.

_____ 8. The soldiers stayed in their line and they did not **waver**. There was no way for the enemy to get through.
    a. a road or surface with an upward slope
    b. to try to persuade or convince
    c. to speed up
    d. vaguely; not clearly
    e. to an extreme
    f. to become unreliable
    g. to refuse or say "no" to something
    h. refusal to do something or accept something

B. Use the new words

Complete the sentences with words from Exercise A. Use correct verb tenses.

1. I asked him to lend me some money, but he _____.

2. Her family _____ her to go to college, and she finally agreed.

3. My mother gets frightened every time the car _____.

4. I _____ remember that house, but I think I was only there once.

5. The doctor said she needed to _____ change her eating habits.

6. He won't change his mind. Once he makes a decision, he never _____.

7. There was a lot of _____ to the schedule change. No one liked the new hours.

8. Look for a flat place to put your tent. If it's on an _____, you'll have trouble sleeping.

V. UNDERSTANDING GRAMMAR: ADJECTIVES AFTER DIRECT OBJECTS

A. Read about adjectives after direct objects

We normally think of adjectives as coming before a noun, as in *the **tall** man*, or after a linking verb like *be*, as in *She is **tired***. But sometimes we place adjectives after direct objects. In this position, the adjective is called "an object complement."

   Notice the adjectives in this excerpt from the reading. Each one is directly after the noun it describes.

   *[I]. . .kept the reins **tight**, my body **still**, my weight **steady** over his shoulders. . .*

B. Identify meanings

Read the sentences. Underline the adjectives. Circle the nouns they describe.

1. I like my coffee black.
2. We painted the house green.
3. His gift made her happy.
4. They considered the new machine useless.
5. Thomas found the work difficult.
6. The tea kept me awake for studying.

C. Use adjectives as object complements

Use the adjectives in the box to complete the following sentences.

> interested
> finished
> angry
> exciting
> cold
> yellow

1. This bag will keep your food _____.

2. I want to paint my bedroom _____.

3. The teacher tells jokes and shows videos to keep the students _____.

4. I hope you like this book. I bought it for you because I found it very _____.

5. Her brother made her _____ when he yelled at her.

6. He submitted the project because he considered it _____.

VI. READ IT AGAIN

Read the passage again. Answer the question.

What mistake did the jockey in front of him make?

_____

Sickness and Health

RULES FOR HEALTHFUL EATING

I. PRE-READING

A. Background information

This excerpt is from the book, *Digestive Wellness*, by Elizabeth Lipski. She believes that many people in America are overfed and undernourished because they eat more than they need to, and they eat highly processed, poor-quality, nutrient-poor foods. She recommends a digestion-enhancing and health supportive diet that relies on natural home-cooked, whole-food meals.

B. Words to know before you read

Match the words to their definitions.

_____ 1. vibrancy   a. overweight; in a way that is unhealthy

_____ 2. ensure   b. having or showing great life, activity, and energy

_____ 3. sustaining   c. to supply with water

_____ 4. obesity   d. agricultural products such as fruits and vegetables

_____ 5. rejuvenate   e. providing what is needed for something or someone to exist

_____ 6. produce   f. to make sure, certain, or safe

_____ 7. hydrate   g. to defend yourself against someone or something

_____ 8. fend (off)   h. to give new strength or energy

_____ 9. pesticide   i. grown without the use of chemicals

_____ 10. organic   j. eating a small amount of food between meals

_____ 11. snacking   k. chemical used to kill insects that damage plants

C. Reading strategy

Quickly read each of the following healthy rules. Then answer the question.

What is the main idea of each rule?

_____   _____

_____   _____

_____   _____

_____   _____

_____   _____

II. READ

Read the text. Mark the words you don't know, but don't stop reading to look them up.

Rules to Eat, Cook, and Live By

Here are 12 rules to help simplify healthful eating. You can tackle them all at once or implement one at a time. Make your home a sanctuary of good eating.

1. **The Life in Foods Gives Us Life**
    Fresh foods have the greatest enzyme activity. Enzymes are to the body what spark plugs are to the engine of a car. If we eat foods with little enzyme activity, they don't "spark" our body to work correctly. Eating foods that have natural vibrancy gives vibrant energy to our own bodies. So if it won't rot or spoil, don't eat it!

2. **Plan Ahead and Carry Food with You**
    Planning ahead and carrying your own food are great tools for healthful eating. Planning helps you create balanced meals and saves shopping time. Carrying snacks for yourself and your kids helps keep your moods and blood sugar levels even. It also saves you money and time, and you can ensure that the snacks are healthful.

3. **Eat Small, Frequent Meals**
    Snacking is a great strategy for boosting and sustaining energy. Snacking keeps blood sugar levels even and facilitates digestion. Make snacking, especially in the midafternoon, a regular part of your life. You'll find that your energy level will stay more constant throughout the day and your mood will be more consistently pleasurable!

4. **Eat When You Are Hungry and Stop When You Are Satisfied**
    Emotional overeating is one of the reasons for obesity in this country. We regularly turn to food when we want love and support. Don't eat if you aren't hungry, but also don't wait until you are overhungry because that's when we lose control and eat the sweetest, fastest foods in sight.

5. **Relax While Eating**
    Many times we don't even stop what we're doing long enough to sit down when we eat. Remember that eating is a time for rejuvenation of body and

spirit and a time to connect with yourself and with those you are eating with. Family meals are important. Turn the television off and have a family dinner almost every night.

6. **Eat Local Foods in Season**
   Local produce is the freshest and has the highest level of nutrients. Put farm stands, community support agriculture (CSA) markets, and farmer's markets into your food-shopping routine. The food quality, freshness, and enzymes are most abundant in local foods eaten in season. Eating foods in season also reduces the amount of pesticide and herbicide we consume.
   * (Foods in Season are foods that are grown in particular season.)

7. **Choose Organically Grown Foods Whenever Possible**
   Organic foods generally have higher nutrient levels because farmers who use organic methods add more nutrients to the soil, knowing that healthy plants can better fend off pests and that the nutrients end up in the crops.

8. **Eat as Many Fruits and Vegetables as Possible**
   The available research on the positive benefits of eating fruits and vegetables is overwhelming. They are chock-full of vitamins, minerals, fiber, and phytochemicals (plant-produced substances) that protect us from heart disease, cancer, degenerative diseases, and other common health problems. We know this, yet only about 23 percent of us eat at least five servings of fruits and vegetables daily. And what's known is that more is even better. Shoot for 8 to 10 and make most of them vegetables!

9. **Eat High-Quality Protein and High-EPA/DHA Seafood, Organically and Sustainably Produced**
   If you choose to eat animal protein, such as poultry, beef, lamb, pork bison, goat, dairy products, eggs, and/or seafood, try to make sure that it is of the best quality possible.

10. **Eat More High-Fiber Foods**
    The richest food sources of fiber are also the four food groups that make up the bulk of a healthful eating plan: whole grains, legumes (all beans except string beans), vegetables, and fruits. Eating whole-grain products is an excellent way to increase your fiber intake.

11. **Drink Lots of Clean Water**
    Our bodies are 70 percent water. If we don't adequately hydrate our cells, they cannot function properly. Moreover, the water we drink and consume in food is an essential carrier, bringing in nutrients and taking away wastes. Drinking plenty of clean, pure water every day is one of the most promising routes to digestive wellness.

12. **Respect Your Own Biochemical Uniqueness**
    The foods that are best for any person are those that agree with that person's body and unique biochemistry. You will probably need to experiment with your own diet and your family's diet to find out what works best for all of you specifically and over the long term. A proper diet ought to make us feel energetic and keep our immune system strong. Our bodies run best on real foods; a natural-foods diet is the ultimate direction in eating for all of us, no matter exactly how we shape it.

Source: *Digestive Wellness*, by Elizabeth Lipski, New York: McGraw-Hill, 2012

III. COMPREHENSION CHECK

Mark the sentences T (True) or F (False).

_____ 1. Fresh foods have the greatest enzyme activity.

_____ 2. Snacking helps keeps blood sugar levels even.

_____ 3. You should always eat when you're not hungry.

_____ 4. Family meals are important.

_____ 5. Produce that is shipped from other parts of the country has the highest level of nutrients.

_____ 6. The freshest foods are the foods in season.

_____ 7. Organic foods generally have higher nutrients.

_____ 8. People should eat small amounts of fruits and vegetables.

_____ 9. Fruits and vegetables have substances that can protect us from diseases.

_____ 10. Legumes, fruits, vegetables, and whole grains are high in fiber.

_____ 11. Our cells don't need much water to function properly.

_____ 12. All people should eat the same diet of natural foods.

IV. VOCABULARY BUILDING

A. Classify words

Find these words in the text, and decide if they are being used as nouns, verbs, or adjectives. Write them in the correct places in the chart.

tackle

implement

ultimate

sanctuary

facilitates

local

abundant

organic

regular

chock-full

unique

nouns	verbs	adjectives

B. Identify meaning

Write words from the chart that can replace the underlined words.

1. I only buy fruits and vegetables that are <u>grown without the use of chemicals</u>.

    _____

2. We created a <u>shelter</u> where animals would be safe.

    _____

3. We are going to <u>carry out</u> the plan to have the children in bed by 8:00 next year.

    _____

4. We didn't want to drive all the way to the city, so we ate at a <u>nearby</u> restaurant.

    _____

5. I'll <u>take on</u> my housework this weekend.

    _____

6. Green vegetables are <u>plentiful</u> in vitamins.

    _____

7. My aunt keeps fit by attending <u>frequent</u> exercise classes.

    _____

8. Reading before bedtime <u>helps</u> in getting the children to relax and get ready to sleep.

    _____

9. His <u>greatest</u> goal is to win a medal at the Olympics.

    _____

10. She is <u>unlike anyone else</u>.

    _____

11. This book is <u>completely full</u> of information.

    _____

C. Analogies

An analogy is a comparison of two things based on their being alike in some way. For example:

The earth's forests function like lungs in a body.

Reread rule 1. Then answer the question.

What is the analogy in rule 1?

_____

V. UNDERSTANDING GRAMMAR

A. Contractions for future with *will*

Affirmative Statement			
subject	***will***	**base form of verb**	
I			
You			
He She It We	will	leave	later.
You			
They			

Negative Statement				
subject	***will***	**not**	**base form of verb**	
I				
You				
He She It	will	not	leave	later.
We				
You				
They				

Contractions		
I'll		
You'll		
He'll She'll It'll You'll	leave	later.
We'll		
They'll		

Contractions			
I			
You			
He She It	won't	leave	later.
You			
We			
They			

Note: Do not use contractions with short answers that are affirmative.

Yes, I will. (Correct)   *Yes, I'll.* (Incorrect)

B. Use the grammar

Rewrite each sentence using the correct contraction.

1. I will not be able to go shopping today.

   _____

2. We will bring snacks to feed the children.

   _____

3. You will have more energy if you eat more consistently throughout the day.

   _____

4. We will eat a family meal once a day.

   _____

5. She will only buy produce that has been grown locally.

   _____

6. He will eat organic food whenever it's possible.

   _____

7. You will increase your fiber intake by eating black beans.

   _____

8. She will try to drink more water.

   _____

VI. READ IT AGAIN

Read the rules again. Answer the questions.

1. Describe the kinds of food that make up a healthy diet.

   _____

2. Why is it important to drink a lot of water?

   _____

HAPPINESS BOOSTERS

I. PRE-READING

A. Background information

Mental Health

This excerpt is from the book *Happier*, by Dr. Ben-Shahar. He has studied the nature of happiness and its effects on mental health. He claims that getting involved in meaningful activities can lead to a happier, more fulfilling life.

B. Words to know before you read

Match the words to their definitions.

_____ 1.	boost	a. spend time doing things that don't require thought or effort
_____ 2.	impacts	b. lacking in energy or will
_____ 3.	mindless	c. to have a direct effect on
_____ 4.	confidence	d. to make weak
_____ 5.	passion	e. strong feeling of enthusiasm
_____ 6.	passive	f. not intellectually challenging
_____ 7.	engaged	g. belief that you can do something well
_____ 8.	vegetate	h. to make full
_____ 9.	replenish	i. to increase
_____ 10.	enervate	j. greatly interested and involved

II. READ

Read the text. Mark the words you don't know, but don't stop reading to look them up.

Happiness Boosters: The Value of Free Time

Engaging in activities that are personally meaningful, impacts our experience in other areas, not directly related to these activities. The confidence, the passion, the sense of fulfillment gained from such experiences spills over to other areas of our lives.

Meaningful and pleasurable activities can function like a candle in a dark room—and just as it takes a small flame or two to light up an entire physical space, one or two happy experiences during an otherwise uninspiring period can transform our general state (of mind). I call these brief but transforming experiences *happiness boosters*—activities, lasting anywhere from a few minutes to a few hours, that provide us with both meaning and pleasure, both future and present benefit.

Happiness boosters can inspire and invigorate us, acting as both a motivational pull and a motivational push. For example, a meaningful weekend outing can change a person's overall experience of life—including the hours spent at work. The outing can be motivating and pull the person through the week, giving her something to look forward to when she gets up for work in the morning. The same happiness booster can then energize her, providing her the push she needs by recharging her motivational stores for the following week.

Ideally, we want our entire day to be filled with happy experiences. This kind of life is not always attainable, though, and it might be that we need to wait until evenings or weekends to pursue activities that provide present and future benefit. One of the common mistakes people make is that in their free time they choose passive hedonism over an active pursuit of happiness. At the end of a hard day at work or in school, they opt to do nothing or to vegetate in front of the television screen rather than engage in activities that are both pleasurable and meaningful. Soon after they engage in their mindless activity, they fall asleep, which further reinforces their belief that when they complete their daily chores they are too tired to do anything challenging. If instead of doing nothing when we come home from work we turn to our hobbies or other activities that challenge us, that we enjoy and that we care about, we are more likely to get a second wind and replenish our emotional bank. As the educator Maria Montessori has written, "To devote oneself to an agreeable task is restful." Happiness boosters, rather than enervating us, lead to ascending levels of energy.

In order to understand the nature of happiness, and for these words to have an impact on your life, you must reflect on what you have just read and look inside yourself.

What are your happiness boosters? What brief activities can rejuvenate you by providing you with both meaning and pleasure?

Source: *Happier*, by Tal Ben-Shahar, New York: McGraw-Hill, 2007

III. COMPREHENSION CHECK

Mark the sentences T (True) or F (False).

1. Engaging in activities that are meaningful have no impact on other experiences. _____

2. Meaningful and pleasurable activities can have positive effects on our minds. _____

3. Happiness boosters are just short activities that last only a few minutes. _____

4. Happiness boosters are invigorating, motivating, and energizing. _____

5. A common mistake people make is to choose a passive activity over an engaging activity that is pleasurable and meaningful. _____

6. To vegetate in front of a television screen is an active pursuit. _____

7. If we engage in a challenging activity after a long day at work, we will become more tired. _____

IV. VOCABULARY BUILDING

A. Multiple meaning words

Many words have multiple meanings. Often you can determine the correct meaning of the word by the context.

Look at how the boldface word in each of the following sentences is used in the context, and circle the definition that best matches the meaning of the word. Keep in mind that all definitions are true definitions for the word in boldface.

1. Engaging in activities that are personally meaningful, impacts our experience in other areas, not directly **related** to these activities.

   a. connected in some way

   b. in the same family

2. The confidence, the passion, the **sense** of fulfillment gained from such experiences spills over to other areas of our lives.

   a. one of the five natural powers (touch, taste, smell, sight, and hearing)

   b. a feeling

3. . . .one or two happy experiences during an otherwise uninspiring period can transform our general **state**.

   a. the condition of a person's mind

   b. to say something

   c. a region of a country

4. I call these **brief** but transforming experiences *happiness boosters*.

   a. a document that states the law

   b. lasting a short period of time

   c. to give instructions

5. . . .we need to wait until evenings or weekends to pursue activities that provide present and future **benefit**.

   a. something extra that is given by an employer, such as vacation time or insurance

   b. a social event

   c. something helpful that promotes well-being

6. One of the **common** mistakes people make is that in their free time they choose passive activities over an active pursuit of happiness.

   a. without special rank or status

   b. frequently happening

7. The same happiness booster can then energize her, providing her the push she needs by recharging her motivational **stores** for the following week.

   a. a large amount or supply of something

   b. a building where things are sold

8. At the end of a hard day at work or in school, they opt to do nothing or to **vegetate** in front of the television screen. . . .

   a. to be passive or inactive

   b. to grow or spread

9.   . . .we are more likely to get a second wind and replenish our emotional **bank**.

   a. a financial institution

   b. a supply or stock held in reserve

   c. to have confidence or faith in

10.   By reflecting on your happiness boosters, you can better understand the **nature** of happiness.

   a. the natural world and everything in it, such as mountains, trees, and animals

   b. a basic quality of something

B. Idioms

get a second wind = get more energy

This idiom is often used with *getting more energy* after already having expended a lot of energy.

> *Although I had worked 10 hours, I got a second wind in the evening.*

Copy the sentence from the text that uses this idiom.

_____

_____

V.   UNDERSTANDING GRAMMAR: TOO

A.   Read about *too*

Too means "to an undesirable degree." It is used before adjectives and adverbs to express a negative meaning. *Not too* expresses a positive meaning when it is used with adjectives and adverbs that are negative qualities.

> *It's **too** hot to play outside.*
> *It's not **too** big to fit through the door.*

Do not confuse *too* and *very*.

> *Too* (undesirable degree)
> *This school is **too** small. There aren't enough students to have two teams.*

> *Very* (great degree)
> *This school is **very** small. Teachers are able to give each student a lot of attention.*

B.   Use the grammar

Circle the word that best completes each sentence.

1.   We're (too / very) tired to go out dancing tonight.

2.   She's (too / very) upset about her test score, and she knows she must study harder next time.

3. The theater is (too / very) crowded, so the show must probably be good.

4. Her daughter is (too / very) young to go on the roller coaster.

5. She's (too / very) poor to afford a new car, so she's looking at used ones.

6. The lemonade is (too / very) sour for him to drink, so he'll drink water.

7. Her mother is (too / very) sweet to offer us dinner.

VI. READ IT AGAIN

Read the passage again. Answer the question.

What is the general message of the excerpt?

_____

_____

_____

MENTAL GREMLINS

I. PRE-READING

A. Background information

This passage is from the book, *Mind Gym: An Athlete's Guide to Inner Excellence*, by Gary Mack. Mack explores the psychological health of athletes and people who have experienced success in many different areas of life. He has determined that mental skills are just as important to performance as physical skills, if not more. In this excerpt, you will read about the importance of thinking positively about yourself, and how negative thoughts can keep you from doing your best.

B. Words to know before you read

Match the words to their definitions.

_____ 1. vitally   a. to stop

_____ 2. essence   b. expressing disapproval or finding fault

_____ 3. diminished   c. render unable to move

_____ 4. discount   d. extremely important

_____ 5. prevent   e. to weaken or make less effective

_____ 6. undermine   f. basic nature of things

_____ 7. paralyze   g. to cause constant worry

_____ 8. plagued   h. lessened

_____ 9. conditional   i. to think of something as having little importance

_____ 10. critical   j. something that will happen only if something else happens

C. Reading strategy

Quickly read the first line of each paragraph. Then answer the question.

What are the seven "gremlins" that prevent athletes from doing their best?

_____   _____

_____   _____

_____   _____

_____

II. READ

Read the text. Mark the words you don't know, but don't stop reading to look them up.

What you think affects how you feel and perform. Training your brain is as important as training your body.

A person's self-concept is vitally important. On his deathbed, Sigmund Freud said the essence of success in life is love and work. As individuals we all want to feel lovable and capable. If you don't feel good about yourself, you tend not to perform well. Those who have a negative self-image find ways to self-destruct. In psychology there is something we call the self-consistency theory. It means we act consistent to our self-concept—our self-image. If you don't see yourself as successful, then your chances of succeeding are diminished. When good things happen, you tend to discount them.

   We all have self-defeating thoughts and behaviors that undermine performance. I call them gremlins, the little invisible creatures that prevent athletes from performing their best. Here's my gremlin checklist.

Fear   We all have a primitive fight-or-flight mechanism built into us to survive. It's a neurochemical response. We are ready to fight or flee whatever is threatening us. In reality, most dangers are not a threat to life or limb. They are a psychological threat to self-esteem and ego. Why else would a brain surgeon turn to jelly over a four-foot downhill breaking putt [a stroke to the hole in golf]? It's a threat to self-image. Fear actually can paralyze you.

Anger   We have to learn to control our emotions or they will control us. Anger is born out of frustration and expectations.

Anxiety   This is a generalized feeling of uncertainty or dread; a sense that something bad is going to happen. We all become anxious, but people plagued by this gremlin get anxious about being anxious. This only leads to trouble.

Self-consciousness   Some athletes are afraid of looking bad or embarrassing themselves. They focus on the image of how they look instead of the task at hand. You can't perform well if you're afraid of embarrassing yourself.

Perfectionism Self-critical, negative perfectionists can never do enough. Their mind-set often is fueled by a fear of failure. Perfectionists often have a very critical, self-condemning voice. I believe perfectionism often comes from conditional parenting. Children internalize criticism. Critical, condemning coaches who use fear and embarrassment injure a young person's psychological health.

Stubbornness Some people are stubborn, unwilling to learn. They're not open to change. They believe the devil they know is better than the devil they don't know. They aren't going to take risks that will help them reach the next level. This is unfortunate because in sports you must learn how to fail successfully.

Lack of motivation Some athletes simply lack the drive to become the best they can be. [*Drive* in this context means, " the impulse to carry on with energy.] You can't buy motivation. You can't obtain it from someone else. "Motivation is something nobody else can give you," Joe DiMaggio said. "Others can help motivate you, but basically it must come from you, and it must be a constant desire to do your very best at all times and under any circumstances."

It is important to look at yourself and identify your gremlins. In sports, as in life, the first step to success is getting out of your own way.

Source: *Mind Gym,* by Gary Mack, New York: McGraw-Hill, 2001

III. COMPREHENSION CHECK

Match the names of the "self-defeating" thoughts and mind-sets with the definitions.

_____ 1. fear

_____ 2. anger

_____ 3. anxiety

_____ 4. self-consciousness

_____ 5. perfectionism

_____ 6. stubbornness

_____ 7. lack of motivation

a. mind-set created by a fear of failure

b. feeling a threat to self-esteem and ego

c. unwilling to learn

d. not having drive to be the best

e. strong feeling of uncertainty

f. focusing on the image of how one looks

g. emotion born from frustration and expectations

IV. VOCABULARY BUILDING

A. Words with the reflexive prefix *self-*

This excerpt contains many words with the reflexive prefix *self-*. Read the following definitions and sentences. Notice that when using the reflexive prefix *self-*, it is always connected to the following word with a hyphen.

self-conscious   *to be aware of oneself, as well as realizing that others are also aware*

*She's always **self-conscious** when she has to give a speech.*

self-critical   *to be disapproving or critical of oneself*

*When he's playing the game, he thinks he makes mistakes, and he's **self-critical**.*

self-condemning   *to express strong disapproval of oneself*

*He makes **self-condemning** comments after he makes mistakes.*

self-defeating   *acting to defeat one's self*

*Thinking you will fail is a **self-defeating** attitude.*

self-destructive   *destroying one's self*

*Drinking in excess every night is **self-destructive**.*

self-esteem   *having respect for yourself and your abilities*

*Having a good relationship with my father helped my **self-esteem**.*

self-image   *the way you think about yourself, your abilities, or appearance*

*She has a poor **self-image**.*

B. Use the new words

Complete the sentences with the boldface words from Exercise A.

1. She doesn't like how her dress fits, and she thinks others will notice how badly it fits. She is _____.

2. His drug abuse shows that he is _____.

3. Before the competition, he thought he would fail. These are _____ thoughts.

4. He thinks his ears are too big and his muscles aren't big enough. He has a poor_____.

5. She's confident about herself, and it shows in how she treats others. She has good _____.

6. He made _____ remarks about how badly he spoke at the meeting.

7. After performing in the show, she was very _____ and counted all the mistakes she had made.

V. UNDERSTANDING GRAMMAR: MODAL VERBS

A. Modal verbs

Can is a modal. A modal is followed by the base form of a verb and has the same form for all subjects. Here are the present and past forms of the five modals in the affirmative and negative:

Present Form Affirmative	Present Form Negative	Past Form Affirmative	Past Form Negative
can	cannot can't	could	could not couldn't
may	may not	might	might not
must	must not mustn't* (not usually used in American English)	X	X
shall	shall not	should	should not shouldn't
will	will not won't	would	would not wouldn't

The present forms have no third-person singular with an added -s. For example:

> *He **can** go.*
> *She **will** leave.*

NOT

> *He can**s** go.*
> *She will**s** leave.*

* *Must* has no past form. It is the only verb in English to have a present but no past.

B. Use the grammar

From the "gremlin checklist" in the passage, find three sentences using the modal can, *and write them in the blanks.*

1. _____

2. _____

3. _____

From the "gremlin checklist" in the passage, find one sentence using the modal can't, *and write it in the blank.*

4. _____

From the "gremlin checklist" in the passage, find one sentence using the modal must, *and write it in the blank.*

5. _____

VI. READ IT AGAIN

Read the passage again. Answer the question.

What is the general message of the passage?

_____

_____

_____

SYMPTOMS OF DEPRESSION

I. PRE-READING

A. Background information

Depression is a growing problem throughout the world. Though depression has often been thought of as an adult sickness, many mental health–care workers, teachers, and parents are beginning to take depression in children and adolescents more seriously. This excerpt is from the book *Why Boys Don't Talk—And Why It Matters*, by Susan Morris Shaffer and Linda Perlman Gordon. It focuses on how parents can recognize depression in adolescents, and in particular, the symptoms of depression that can be displayed in young boys.

B. Words to know before you read

Match the word with its definition.

_____ 1. vulnerable

_____ 2. aggression

_____ 3. indicate

_____ 4. tension

_____ 5. chronic

_____ 6. isolates

_____ 7. rigid

_____ 8. permissive

_____ 9. indifference

_____ 10. tolerance

_____ 11. intensity

_____ 12. maintaining

a. angry or violent behavior or feelings

b. continuing or occurring again and again

c. giving people a lot of freedom to do what they want

d. easily hurt physically, mentally, or emotionally

e. not easily changed

f. great energy, enthusiasm, seriousness, or effort

g. lack of interest or concern about something

h. to show or suggest (something)

i. accepting different feelings, habits, or beliefs

j. keeping

k. to put or keep in a place that is separate from others

l. a feeling of nervousness, excitement, or fear

C. Reading strategy

Scan the text, then answer the question.

What is the main idea of this excerpt?

_____

II. READ

Read the text. Mark the words you don't know, but don't stop reading to look them up.

How Vulnerable Is My Teen to Depression?

How can you identify the root causes of a child's depression and steer him toward help? Since much of adolescent depression is a reaction to a combination of stress factors, you can begin by considering the following questions. Be alert to the fact that several yes answers in combination over the past year can indicate that your child is especially vulnerable to depression.

1. Has your child experienced the loss of an important family member or friend during the last year?

2. Have you and your spouse had significant marital problems resulting in prolonged conflict or tension?

3. Are you and your child's other parent divorced? If so, is your child often asked to relay messages from one parent to the other? Have you communicated to your son that he's now the man of the house?

4. Has your child switched schools with little or no access to old friends?

5. Does your teenager have a chronic illness that limits his activity and/or isolates him?

6. Do you have high expectations of your child and find yourself disappointed—allowing your child to know that he failed to reach your expectation?

7. Is someone in your family very critical of your son? Is he often referred to as the "difficult one"?

8. Are you a strict or rigid parent with a low tolerance for conflict or disagreements?

9. Are you overly permissive, with very few rules and regulations?

10. Do you communicate either verbally or nonverbally that expressing anger is not tolerated in your home?

11. Does your teenager seem to often be the target of criticism, teasing, or indifference from peers?

12. Does your teenager have difficulty making and maintaining friendships?

Be aware that boys act out depression through many behaviors, some of which look different from classical depression. Even if your son isn't especially vulnerable to depression based on the above questions, pay close attention to any symptoms of depression you may notice, including:

- Fatigue
- Loss of pleasure in activities he previously enjoyed
- Increased intensity
- Increased aggression
- New interest in "self-medication" (alcohol or drugs)
- Shift in interest level in sexual encounters
- Harsh self-criticism
- Difficulty concentrating
- Denial of pain
- Overinvolvement with academic work or sports

Source: *Why Boys Don't Talk—And Why It Matters*, by Susan Morris Shaffer and Linda Perlman Gordon, New York: McGraw-Hill, 2005

III. COMPREHENSION CHECK

Read each question. Circle the best answer.

1. This excerpt is about how to identify depression in people in which age group?

    a. teens/adolescents

    b. elderly

2. What can help you identify if your child is vulnerable to depression?

    a. focusing on your child's appearance

    b. considering your child's stress factors

3. Which of the following is more likely to cause depression?

    a. loss of an important family member

    b. losing a card game

4. According to the excerpt, which could be a symptom of depression?

    a. difficulty with making plans with friends

    b. difficulty concentrating on homework

5. According to the excerpt, which is <u>not</u> a symptom of depression?

    a. fatigue

    b. doing well at sports

IV. VOCABULARY BUILDING

A. Verbs and nouns

These words can be used as verbs or nouns. Write one word in each sentence. Use correct verb form.

alert	shift	access	switch	steer	stress

1. **a.** He works on the night _____.

    b. He _____ his ideas later in life.

2. **a.** We couldn't _____ the house through the back.

    b. There's no _____ to the lake if you drive down this street.

3. **a.** We have to _____ the police about the lost dog.

    b. The nurse kept _____ for any change in the patient's condition.

4. **a.** We tried to _____ the cart in a different direction.

    b. _____ are raised on farms in Wisconsin.

5. **a.** Her poor relationship with her manager is causing her a lot of _____.

    b. The dentist _____ the importance of flossing your teeth.

6. **a.** The light _____ is on the wall.

    b. I _____ doctors last year.

B. Idioms

the man of the house = chief male in the house, or man in charge of the house and responsible for taking care of the family

This idiom often refers to a son who becomes the head of a household due to the displacement of a father because of death, divorce, or having to go off to work someplace far away.

Copy the sentence from the text with this idiom.

_____

V. UNDERSTANDING GRAMMAR: THE PRESENT PERFECT

A. Read about the present perfect

The name "present perfect" can be confusing because it's a tense that deals with the past, not the present. The present perfect joins the past with the present. It deals with actions or states that took place continuously or repeatedly in the past and have continued up to the present time. These actions may or may not continue into the future.

> He **has lived** here for five years.
> She **has worked** in the same city since 2012.

Affirmative Statements			
subject	***have/has***	**past participle**	
I	have		
You			
He She It	has	traveled flown	to Chicago.
We	have		
You			
They			

Yes/No Questions			
have/has	**subject**	**past participle**	
Have	you	traveled flown	to Chicago?
Has	he/she/it		
Have	they		

- The past participle of a regular verb has the same form as the simple past: verb + -d/-ed.
- Irregular verbs have different past participle forms. Here is an example of six common irregular verbs and their past tenses:

Base Form	Simple Past	Past Participle
be	was/were	been
bring	brought	brought
cut	cut	cut
fly	flew	flown
go	went	gone

B. Use the present perfect

Using the following table, create eight logical sentences in the present perfect: four affirmative statements, and four questions.

subject	have/has	past participle	
she/he	have	was/were	for a long time
you	has	taught	to the movies
we		learned	English
they		went	sick

1. _____
2. _____
3. _____
4. _____
5. _____
6. _____
7. _____
8. _____

VI. READ IT AGAIN

Read the article again. Answer the question.

What are three stress factors that could cause depression?

1. _____
2. _____
3. _____

9

Children and Parents

POSITIVE PARENTING

I. PRE-READING

A. Background information

This brief is from the book *Why Boys Don't Talk—And Why It Matters*, by Susan Morris Shaffer and Linda Perlman Gordon. It lays out thirteen principles of good parenting.

B. Words to know before you read

Match the words to their definitions.

_____ 1. predictable

_____ 2. reliable

_____ 3. consistent

_____ 4. regardless

_____ 5. investment

a. always acting or behaving in the same way

b. without being stopped or affected by (something)

c. the act of giving your time or effort in order to accomplish something or make something better

d. able to be trusted to do or provide what is needed

e. capable of being known before happening

C. Reading strategy

Quickly scan the parenting brief. Then answer the question.

Who will benefit from *positive parenting*—the parents, children, or both?

_____

II. READ

Read the brief. Mark the words you don't know, but don't stop reading to look them up.

Positive Parenting

The Law of Return

"One good parent is worth 1, 000 schoolmasters."

—Chinese Proverb

The purpose of this parent brief is to present 13 principles of positive parenting.

1. Parenting is a process. You never arrive with all the skills that you need.
2. Parents are not trained to be parents; kids are not trained to be kids. Kids train parents; parents train kids.
3. It is more challenging to be a parent than to function in your job.
4. Parenting is a journey, not a destination.
5. Parents are the most significant influence in a child's life.
6. A parent is the greatest teacher a child will ever have. A parent and child certainly have the longest teaching relationship ever known.
7. It is not a question of whether a parent is a teacher or not, it's a question of what is taught. Parents teach kids a whole language before they come to school.
8. If you pay attention to your child, he will teach you what you need to learn.
9. Parent modeling that includes the unspoken as well as the spoken word is the most powerful force in shaping a child's life.
10. How you spend your time and money tells your kids what you value, regardless of what you say.
11. Successful parenting is predictable, reliable, and consistent.
12. There's no greater investment in life than children.
13. Parents who praise each of their children at least twice a day maintain a positive relationship regardless of the problems they encounter.

Source: *Why Boys Don't Talk—And Why It Matters,* by Susan Morris Shaffer and Linda Perlman Gordon, New York: McGraw-Hill, 2005

III. COMPREHENSION CHECK

Circle the letter of the sentences with the same meaning as the first sentence.

1. Parenting is a process. You never arrive with all the skills that you need.

    a. You learn the skills of parenting over time.

    b. Everyone knows the skills of parenting before becoming a parent.

2. It is more challenging to be a parent than to function in your job.

   a. A job is harder than parenting.

   b. Parenting is harder than a job.

3. Parenting is a journey, not a destination.

   a. The importance of parenting is what you do along the way, not the final result.

   b. The importance of parenting is the final result, not what you do along the way.

4. If you pay attention to your child, he will teach you what you need to learn.

   a. You can learn how to be a parent by paying attention to your child.

   b. You can learn how to be a parent by reading books about parenting.

5. Parent modeling that includes the unspoken as well as the spoken word is the most powerful force in shaping a child's life.

   a. Parents' actions are much more important than their words in shaping a child's life.

   b. Parents' actions and words are extremely important in shaping a child's life.

6. How you spend your time and money tells your kids what you value, regardless of what you say.

   a. Teaching a child what you value can be done by a simple explanation.

   b. Children learn what you value by seeing the way you spend your time and money, not by what you tell them you value.

IV. VOCABULARY BUILDING

A. Using new words

Read the words and their definitions. Then complete the sentences that follow with one of the words from the list.

principles	*rules or beliefs that helps you know what is right and wrong and that influences your actions*
function	*to work or operate*
encounter	*have to experience*
proverb	*a brief popular saying that gives advice about how people should live*
destination	*a place to which a person is going*
significant	*very important*
influence	*the power to change or affect someone or something*

1. I cannot _____ after working for nine hours straight.

2. Have you ever had an _____ with a mean dog?

3. London, England is my final _____.

4. Our team made _____ improvements this year.

5. The children tried to _____ me into buying them candy.

6. At the beginning of each class, she writes a _____ on the board.

V. UNDERSTANDING GRAMMAR: HOMONYMS AND HOMOPHONES

A *homonym* is a word that is spelled and pronounced like another word but is different in meaning. A *homophone* is a word that is pronounced like another word but is different in meaning, origin, or spelling. Here are some homonyms and homophones from this article:

Homonyms:

Word	Definition 1	Definition 2	Definition 3
positive	(adj.) having a good effect: favorable	electricity: (adj.) having more protons than electrons	mathematics: (adj.) greater than zero
return	(v.) to come or go to a place again	(n.) the profit from labor, investment or business	tennis: (v.) to hit back a ball
brief	(adj.) lasting a short time	(n.) a brief statement or report	(v.) to provide a concise summary
kid	(n.) a child	(n.) a young goat	(v.) to speak to someone in a joking way
function	(n.) the special purpose of an activity	(n.) a large ceremony or social event	(v.) to work or operate

Homophones:

principle: (n.) a rule or belief that helps you know what is right and wrong and that influences your actions	principal: (n.) person in charge of a school
whether: (conj.) if it is or was true that. . .	weather: (n.) the temperature and other outside conditions
whole: (adj.) complete or full	hole: (n.) an opening into or through something
taught: (v.) past tense of *teach*	taut: (adj.) very tight from being pulled or stretched
praise: (v.) to say or write good things about someone or something	prays: (v.) to speak to God in order to give thanks or to ask for something

1. *In the Homonym table, circle the definition that matches the word used in the excerpt.*

2. *In the Homophone table, circle the word used in the excerpt.*

VI. READ IT AGAIN

Choose two of the principles from the reading and explain why they are examples of "positive parenting."

1. _____

2. _____

THE POWER OF EARLY EXPERIENCE

I. PRE-READING

A. Background information

This passage is from the book, *The No-Cry Picky Eater Solution*, by Elizabeth Pantley. She offers strategies and advice on how parents can create healthy food habits for children that can last a lifetime.

B. Words to know before you read

Match the words to their definitions.

_____ 1. resistance   a. to set up or bring something about

_____ 2. accustomed   b. ice cream served with toppings

_____ 3. establish   c. a behavior pattern formed by frequent repetition

_____ 4. instill   d. refusal to accept something new or different

_____ 5. sundae   e. in good condition; solid

_____ 6. reserved   f. familiar with something so it seems normal

_____ 7. sound   g. existing or happening before

_____ 8. previously   h. kept or set apart for particular use

_____ 9. habit   i. to gradually have someone to have (an attitude or feeling, etc.)

C. Reading strategy

Scan the list of food routines, and answer the question.

A *vicious cycle* is a repeating situation when one bad action or behavior causes another problem, which makes the first one worse. Why is it a "vicious cycle" to give a child whatever he wants to eat when he resists healthy food?

_____

_____

_____

II. READ

Read the passage. Mark the words you don't know, but don't stop reading to look them up.

The Power of Early Experience

As you try to feed your child a balanced, healthy diet, it can be quite a challenge to battle all that nature throws in front of you. Many parents, coming up against a wall of resistance over and over again, simply give up and feed the child whatever it is he will eat. The problem with this approach is that it becomes a vicious cycle. Your child won't eat healthy food; you feed him the nutrient-poor substitutes; he becomes accustomed to these foods; he won't eat the healthy food you offer. By the time your child outgrows these dietary limitations, his food habits are set in place and harder to change.

Research shows that food preferences are established early in life. Researchers discovered that the foods the children liked at age two or three were usually the same foods they were eating at age 10. This gives parents a tremendous amount of power and responsibility to shape their children's future in previously unrecognized ways. It speaks loudly to the fact that we should use great care in choosing the types of foods we feed our children from a young age.

Create Smart Habits

Kids are naturally wired to follow daily routines and rituals. Whatever they do every day, they will continue to do every day. So work hard to instill some great eating habits. Once they're established, you'll find your child automatically following these patterns. Here are a few sample food routines to consider. These ideas can get you thinking about your own family's routines:

- Eat breakfast every day. One step better—eat something from each food group at breakfast: grains, fruit or vegetable, dairy, and protein.

- Fruit or vegetables are the go-to snack if you are hungry before a meal.

- Sugary desserts (like ice cream sundaes, cake, or pie) are rare but wonderful experiences, typically for special occasions like birthdays, vacations, or holidays.

- Lunch and dinner always include at least one vegetable.

- Added butter, sugar, ketchup, syrups, and sauces are used in small doses.

- Soda pop is a rarely served beverage, perhaps reserved for parties or dining out.

- Water is on the table at every meal.

These are examples of great lifetime habits, since they are all based on sound nutritional theories. Decide which of them you are going to adopt in your family, and add some of your own as well. Remember, kids learn best by example, so be the leader.

Source: *The No-Cry Picky Eater Solution*, by Elizabeth Pantley, New York: McGraw-Hill, 2012

III. COMPREHENSION CHECK

Write answers to the questions.

1. At what point in a person's life are food preferences established?

   _____

2. Why are routines necessary for children?

   _____

3. How often should you eat breakfast?

   _____

4. Which snacks should you eat if you're hungry before a meal?

   _____

5. When should you serve sugary desserts?

   _____

6. At which meals should vegetables be served?

   _____

7. When should soda pop be served?

   _____

8. How often should water be served?

   _____

IV. VOCABULARY BUILDING

A. Understanding from context

Read the sentences and decide if the boldface words are verbs, nouns, or adjectives. Write them in the correct places in the chart.

1. It can be quite a challenge to **battle** all that nature throws in front of you.
2. The problem with this approach is that it becomes a vicious **cycle**.
3. Research shows that food **preferences** are established early in life.
4. By the time your child outgrows these **dietary** limitations, his food habits are set in place and harder to change.
5. This gives parents a tremendous amount of power and responsibility to **shape** their children's future.
6. These ideas can get you thinking about your own family's **routines**.
7. These are examples of great lifetime habits, since they are all based on sound **nutritional** theories.
8. Decide which of them you are going to **adopt** in your family, and add some of your own as well.

verb	adjective	noun

B. Use the new words

Complete the sentences with the boldface words from Exercise A.

1. She did not choose to _____ his approach to feeding children unhealthy food.

2. The _____ guidelines provide nutrition information and advice on healthy foods to eat.

3. He tries to _____ his students into thoughtful and caring people.

4. The things we like to do most, and the foods we like to eat most, are our _____.

5. I have many different _____ that I follow daily.

6. After feeding children healthy foods for a while, it becomes less of a _____ to get them to choose healthy foods on their own.

7. A _____ is a series of events that happens repeatedly.

8. There is nothing _____ in soda pop.

C. Idioms

Go-to = reliable

This idiom is often used with a person or thing that is most trusted.

The *go-to person* on a sports team is someone that can be relied upon to perform well.

The *go-to source* for online hotel reviews would be the most trusted site for the reviews.

Copy the sentence from the text that uses this idiom.

_____

V. UNDERSTANDING GRAMMAR: *COUNT AND NONCOUNT NOUNS*

A. Read about vount and noncount nouns

Knowing the difference between count and noncount nouns will help you to use the noun plural ending -s correctly; use the appropriate article, that is, *the, a,* or *an;* and use words that express quantities, such as *many, several, a few, few,* and *many.*

Count nouns:

Count nouns are nouns that can be counted. They can be either singular or plural nouns:

one **car**   four **cars**

A, *an*, *the*, *a number*, or *no article* can come before count nouns.

Count nouns are pluralized by adding -s or -es to the singular form.

Noncount nouns:

Noncount nouns are nouns that cannot be counted.

Noncount nouns are always singular. They cannot be pluralized, and therefore they cannot have an **-s** added to the end.

The or *no article* can come before noncount nouns.

Count Nouns			
a, an, the, number, **or (no article)**	**count noun**	**verb**	
A(n) The One	car	is	fast.
The Four	cars	are	clean.
(no article)	Cars	are	safe.

Noncount Nouns			
the **or no article**	**noncount nouns**	**verb**	
The	juice	is	fresh.
(no article)	Juice	is	sweet.

B. Identify count and noncount nouns

Find count and noncount nouns from the passage, and place them in the correct columns.

Count Nouns	Noncount Nouns

VI. READ IT AGAIN

Read the tips again. Answer the questions.

1. According to the passage, why is it important to establish healthy food routines when children are young?

   _____

2. What are three healthy food routines?

   _____

HOUSEHOLD CHORES

I. PRE-READING

A. Background information

This passage is from the book *Raising a Self-Disciplined Child*, by Robert Brooks, PhD, and Sam Goldstein, PhD. The book is about how to help your child become more responsible, confident, and resilient. This passage offers advice on how parents can get their children to help with the household chores without having to nag or punish.

B. Words to know before you read

Match the words to their definitions.

_____ 1. practical   a. willing to be helpful by doing what someone asks for

_____ 2. tedious   b. intending to punish

_____ 3. eager   c. boring and long

_____ 4. nagging   d. useful and reasonable

_____ 5. procrastination   e. delaying something that should be done; to put off

_____ 6. punitive   f. to annoy with repeated requests

_____ 7. strategy   g. very excited and interested

_____ 8. cooperative   h. a careful plan

C. Reading strategy

Read the text. Then answer the question.

This passage can be understood as a response to parents' frustrations and questions about getting children involved in household chores. What is the parents' question the authors are addressing?

_____

_____

II. READ

Read the text. Mark the words you don't know, but don't stop reading to look them up.

As a practical matter, even if we are careful to express to our children that we need their help for the household to run more smoothly, many responsibilities still seem boring or tedious. How many of us are eager to clean our room, clear the dishes, or take out the garbage? These are the kinds of activities that result in procrastination or "forgetting," which leads to nagging and punitive forms of discipline. Parents often ask, "What can we do so that our kids complete these chores without our nagging?" These are steps you can take to help to get things done and prevent discipline problems.

1. Talk about why the tasks have to be done. Discuss with your children why certain activities are important and what would occur if they weren't done.

2. Have a family meeting about what needs to be done. Sit down as a family, and list the household responsibilities. Often differences of opinion arise about what responsibilities are important. These differences can serve as the basis for further dialogue among family members. Some chores judged important at one point may later be discarded. Once a list of responsibilities is complete, your family can review which items must be done by certain members of the household and which can be done by any family member.

3. Figure out who does what, when, and for how long. When your list of responsibilities is done and prioritized, your family can develop a system for how these responsibilities should be delegated and for what length of time. Some families design a rotating schedule so that chores among family members change every week or month.

4. Agree on a way to remind everyone of chores. Even with the aid of a written list and rotating chores, children (and even parents) may forget to meet their responsibilities. Discuss what the family should do if anyone, including parents, neglects to fulfill a responsibility.

Whatever the strategy you use, involve your children in understanding why everyone in the family needs to help and how the work can be distributed fairly. While parents can reserve the final say, children will appreciate their role in family life if they believe their views are being heard. When this occurs, they are more likely to be cooperative and responsible, and you will have helped to develop self-discipline.

Source: *Raising a Self-Disciplined Child*, by Robert Brooks, PhD and Sam Goldstein, PhD, New York: McGraw-Hill, 2007

III. COMPREHENSION CHECK

Place a check mark by the actions the writers list to help get kids to complete chores and prevent discipline problems.

1. _____ Talk about why the tasks have to be done.

2. _____ Make your child do the task quickly.

3. _____ Have a family meeting.

4. _____ Discuss why certain activities are important.

5. _____ As a family, list household responsibilities.

6. _____ Prioritize the responsibilities.

7. _____ Design a rotating schedule.

8. _____ Agree on a way to remind everyone of the chores.

9. _____ Punish anyone who doesn't do the chores.

10. _____ Reward everyone who does a chore.

11. _____ Discuss what to do if someone doesn't do the chores.

IV. VOCABULARY BUILDING

A. Understanding from context

The following words are all verbs. Read the verbs and definitions. Then write the correct verb in the sentences that follow.

prevent	*to stop*
prioritize	*to organize so that the most important thing is done first*
discard	*to throw away*
delegate	*to give responsibility to someone*
neglect	*to fail to do something*
involve	*to include*
distribute	*to give out*
reserve	*to hold or keep back*

1. They couldn't _____ the tasks without knowing which one was the most important.

2. She wants to _____ all of her clothes that no longer fit.

3. He tried to _____ the accident by swerving off the road.

4. They _____ their children in everything they do.

5. The parents _____ the hardest chores to the older children of the family.

6. The coach _____ uniforms to each member of the team.

7. If you _____ to brush your teeth, you may get cavities.

8. She is trying to _____ criticism of her children's mistakes.

V. UNDERSTANDING GRAMMAR: IMPERATIVES

<u>A.</u> Read about imperatives

An imperative sentence tells a person to do something.
   It is understood that the subject of an imperative is *you*, even though we don't write it or say it.

> *Drive carefully.*   *Open the door.*

Imperatives have the same form whether we are talking to one person or more than one person.

> Parent to child: *Sit down, please.*   Parent to group of children:
> *Sit down, please.*

Imperative sentences are punctuated with a period or exclamation point.

Examples:

   Giving commands: *Take out the garbage!*

   Giving advice: *Have a family meeting about what needs to be done.*

   Making requests: *Take your shoes off when entering the house.*

   Giving directions: *Turn left at the light.*

   Giving instructions: *First, draw the shape. Then, cut out the shape.*

   Giving warnings: *Be careful! The dogs bite.*

   Making offers: *Help yourself to the apple pie.*

<u>B.</u> Identify imperatives

Write six imperatives from the passage.

1. _____

2. _____

3. _____

4. _____

5. _____

6. _____

VI. READ IT AGAIN

Answer the question.

Why should parents involve their children in making decisions about the household chores?

_____

_____

ESTABLISHING YOURSELF AS COACH

I. PRE-READING

<u>A.</u> Background information

This excerpt is from the book *Coaching Youth Soccer: The Baffled Parent's Guide*, by Bobby Clark. He offers advice on how parents can coach their children's teams successfully, meaning teaching children the basics of soccer as well as the fun and rewards of the game.

<u>B.</u> Words to know before you read

Match the words to their definitions.

_____ 1. establish	a. to lose or give up something
_____ 2. instill	b. the surrounding environment
_____ 3. forfeit	c. a way of behaving that shows a willingness to obey rules
_____ 4. signal	d. showing someone how something is done
_____ 5. discipline	e. a shape that has a pointed top and sides that form a circle at the bottom
_____ 6. distraction	f. to set up or put into place
_____ 7. demonstration	g. rate, rhythm, or pattern of an activity
_____ 8. push-up	h. something that makes it difficult to pay attention
_____ 9. cone	i. to gradually cause someone to have an attitude or feeling
_____ 10. tempo	j. a sound or nonverbal gesture that tells someone to do something
_____ 11. atmosphere	k. exercise in which you lay on your stomach and raise your lower body by pushing up and lowering down with your arms

C. Reading strategy

Quickly read the first line of each paragraph. Then answer the question.

What is the topic of each section?

_____

_____

_____

_____

_____

_____

II. READ

Read the text. Mark the words you don't know, but don't stop reading to look them up.

Establishing Yourself as Coach

Creating an Atmosphere of Good Habits

One of the most important things you can do as a coach is to instill good habits in your players. By teaching them to attend to the little things, such as getting to practice on time and coming with their soccer balls properly inflated and their equipment well cared for, they will start taking care of these details at the games—and perhaps in life as well. Players will learn to work as part of a team, and since this may well be the first time your players will be a part of a team, instilling good habits in them now lays a strong foundation for the future.

Keep It Fun

You can help your players learn good habits only if they respect you and your position. Kids respond best to authority if they can have fun while they are learning what you expect of them, and if they are a part of the process. The best way to do this is to make everything a game. I've found that kids respond well to little forfeits that everyone enjoys. For example, if you want the team to come in from the field or to pick up all the cones, give them a challenge, and ask them how long it will take them to finish the job. They come up with the challenge for themselves: they may say they can pick up the cones in 30 seconds. Make it a contest: if they can get the cones in 25 seconds, they win, and you will do 10 push-ups. If you win, they do 10 pushups. The task becomes a game, and you're a part of it—they can catch you the same as you can catch them. They are learning to take responsibility for their actions, and learning this valuable lesson can be done in a fun way.

Let Your Signal Be Their Guide

Your players will need to learn to listen to you and to respond to your signal. When you want them to listen, speak in a quiet voice—when you speak in a loud voice, their volume will rise to meet your voice. Speak to them softly, or don't even speak at all—when someone is not paying attention and you stop speaking, your silence will get the message across. Then everyone refocuses on you, and you can carry on.

Set a Good Example

The coach has to set standards—if you expect your kids to play like a team, to pay attention, and to focus on the sport, your discipline has to be the best of everyone's. You have to be dressed to play, ready to play, and focused on what you are doing even more than your players.

Be Aware of the Environment around You

When you want your players to focus on you, be aware of other distractions—such as other practices or games. Position yourself and the demonstrations so that the kids are looking away from other distractions. You can repeatedly bring them in close around you, but this takes a lot of time. I'm a strong believer in keeping a good tempo during practice. Bring your players in close enough so they can hear you, but don't waste time stopping and bringing them in just to send them out again. If it's a strong wind, bring them in closer so they can hear, and if it's a low sun, be careful where you position yourself so they aren't looking into the sun to see you.

Assess Their Attention Span

You will need to learn how long your players can pay attention without getting bored or restless. The biggest mistake you can make is to do all the talking or demonstrating. I watched a camp in New Jersey many years ago. The head coach was working hard, and as the day wore on, the coach enjoyed doing the demonstrations more and more. It ended up that the kids were moving for about 30 seconds or so, and then the coach was demonstrating for 3 minutes, and it wasn't clear who was having a good time—the coach or the kids. The players are the ones who need the practice. Keep that in mind.

Source: *Coaching Youth Soccer: The Baffled Parent's Guide*, by Bobby Clark, New York: McGraw-Hill, 2000

III. COMPREHENSION CHECK

Mark the main idea of the title for each section.

_____ 1. Creating an Atmosphere of Good Habits

a. make everything a game or a challenge

_____ 2. Keep It Fun

b. understand ways in which your players can be distracted

_____ 3. Let Your Signal Be Their Guide

c. your own behaviors best show players how you expect them to act

____ 4. Set a Good Example   d. keep players active so they stay focused

____ 5. Be Aware of the Environment around You   e. teach players to listen to you

____ 6. Assess Their Attention Span   f. teach your players good habits and to work as a team

IV. VOCABULARY BUILDING

A. Classify words

Find these words in the text, and decide if they are nouns, verbs, or adjectives. Write them in the correct places in the chart.

assess

set

attend to

inflated

respect

habits

valuable

authority

refocus

position

nouns	verbs	adjectives

B. Identify meaning

Write words from the chart that can replace the underlined words.

1. For safety reasons, you must <u>place</u> yourself behind the police barricade.

_____

2. Reading to children when they are very young creates good reading <u>practices</u>.

_____

3. His advice is <u>priceless</u>.

_____

4. They <u>admire</u> their coach greatly, and listen to her criticism.

_____

5. These balls have not been <u>filled with air</u>.

   _____

6. She will not be able to <u>devote her time to</u> the new patients.

   _____

7. He has the <u>power to give orders</u> since he is the headmaster of the school.

   _____

8. She <u>determined and fixed</u> the time limit for each task.

   _____

9. We tried to <u>estimate</u> how much damage had been done by the storm.

   _____

10. The children could not <u>concentrate again</u> on their homework after the big party.

    _____

V. UNDERSTANDING GRAMMAR: IDIOMATIC PREPOSITIONS

A. Read about idiomatic prepositions

You may hear idiomatic prepositions often, but using them correctly can be tricky. Idioms are particular to a given language; they even differ between American English and British English. Idioms are phrases that cannot be understood by defining each individual word in the phrase. Here are some prepositional idioms in American English:

Incorrect	Correct
according *with* the plan	according *to* the plan
apologize *about*	apologize *for*
capable *for*	capable *of*
concerned *to*	concerned *about*
interested *about*	interested *in*
jealous *for* others	jealous *of* others
on mind	*in* mind
puzzled *on*	puzzled *at, by*

B. Use the grammar

Write the correct preposition for the idiom to complete the sentence.

1. According _____ the map, we need to drive south.

2. They apologized _____ being late.

3. She's capable _____ tying her own shoes, but she likes someone else to do it.

4. We're not concerned _____ children coloring out of the lines.

5. She's interested _____ many different sports.

6. They're jealous _____ the other team's new equipment.

7. For the role of the villain, I had no one in particular _____ mind.

8. He's puzzled _____ his manager's negative report.

VI.   READ IT AGAIN

Read the paragraphs again. Answer the questions.

1. Who is responsible for setting a good example?

   _____

2. What is the best way to keep children from getting bored or restless?

   _____

10

Free Time, Fun Time

VISITING THRIFT STORES

I. PRE-READING

A. Background information

Shopping can be a fun and relaxing way to spend your free time. This brief excerpt is from the book *Style on a Shoestring*, by Andy Paige. Doing something "on a shoestring" means you do it with very little money. This excerpt is about thrift store shopping. Thrift stores sell used clothing.

B. Words to know before you read

Match the words to their definitions.

_____ 1. sap

_____ 2. thrifty

_____ 3. garment

_____ 4. caveat

_____ 5. epitomizes

_____ 6. diva

_____ 7. devoted

_____ 8. charity

a. a warning to be remembered when you are doing something

b. to weaken

c. wise and careful use of money so it's not wasted

d. being a perfect example

e. a successful woman who is attractive and fashionable

f. an organization that helps people who are poor

g. piece of clothing

h. having a strong love or loyalty

C. Reading strategy

Quickly read the excerpt. Then answer the question.

When shopping at a thrift store, what will you have to spend more of, money or time?

_____

II. READ

Read the text. Mark the words you don't know, but don't stop reading to look them up.

Thrift stores can be a creative field of dreams for the devoted shopper hero. A thrift store will sap your time, but it'll never sap your dinero. Thrift stores are usually connected to a charity and take in donated items in any ol' condition. If you are lucky, things are organized by color and garment type, but a boutique it ain't.

As you know, you have to spend a little more time if you plan on spending less money, and a thrift store epitomizes this principle. Every thrifty diva I know has a fabulous thrift store find in her closet with a needle-in-a-haystack tale to tell, but you've got to be up for the hunt. Thrift store items will need to be cleaned, they can't be returned, and many stores do not offer fitting rooms. One easy way around this little caveat is to shop in a thin tee and skirt, so you can slip on tops and easily try on bottoms.

Source: *Style on a Shoestring*, by Andy Paige, New York: McGraw-Hill, 2009

III. COMPREHENSION CHECK

Mark the sentences T (True) or F (False).

_____ 1. It takes a lot of time to shop at thrift stores.

_____ 2. It takes a lot of money to shop at thrift stores.

_____ 3. Thrift stores sell clothing that has been bought from top designers.

_____ 4. Thrift stores sell clothing that has been donated.

_____ 5. Thrift store items are always clean.

_____ 6. Thrift store items need to be cleaned.

_____ 7. You may not return items bought at thrift stores.

_____ 8. You can always try on clothes in fitting rooms at thrift stores.

IV. VOCABULARY BUILDING

A. Understanding from context

Read the sentences. Before you look up words in the dictionary, use the context of each sentence to help you match the boldface words and idioms with the definitions that follow.

_____ 1. Thrift stores can be a creative **field of dreams** for the devoted shopper hero.

_____ 2. If you are lucky, things are organized by color and garment type, but a **boutique** it ain't.

_____ 3. Every thrifty diva I know has a fabulous thrift store **find** in her closet.

_____ 4. Every thrifty diva I know has a fabulous thrift store find in her closet with a **needle-in-a-haystack** tale to tell.

_____ 5. You've got to be up for the **hunt**.

_____ 6. Shop in a thin **tee** and skirt.

_____ 7. So you can slip on tops and easily try on **bottoms**.
   a. search
   b. clothes for below your waist
   c. something valuable that has been found or discovered
   d. something that's almost impossible to find
   e. a light shirt
   f. reference to a movie with a fairy-tale ending
   g. small stylish store that usually sells expensive things

B. American slang

   ol' = old
   ain't = "am not," "are not," "is not," "have not," or "has not"

These two words are examples of American slang.

Copy the phrases from the text that uses these slang words.

_____

C. Phrasal verbs for shopping

There are several phrasal verbs we use when we talk about shopping and clothing. Match the phrasal verbs on the left with the definitions on the right.

_____ 1. to pick out something/ to pick something out

_____ 2. to shop around

_____ 3. to grow out of something

_____ 4. to grow into something

_____ 5. to put on something/to put something on

_____ 6. to try on something/to try something on

_____ 7. to ring up something/to ring something up

_____ 8. to break in something/ to break something in

_____ 9. to browse/browsing

a. to grow too big for something

b. to compare prices at different stores

c. to select or choose

d. to wear clothing briefly to check for fit and comfort

e. to complete a transaction at the cash register

f. to wear something until it becomes comfortable, such as leather footwear

g. to just look around

h. to wear something

i. to grow big enough to fit into something

V.   UNDERSTANDING GRAMMAR: COORDINATING CONJUNCTIONS

A. Read about coordinating conjunctions.

To connect two sentences, use a comma + a coordinating conjunction.

The following words are coordinating conjunctions. The acronym, FANBOYS, can help you remember them:

For

And

Nor

But

Or

Yet

So

* The coordinating conjunction *nor* is not used that often. Its most common use is in the correlative pair *neither. . .nor*.

That's **neither** what I said **nor** what I meant.

*The word *for* is also not used that often as a coordinating conjunction. It sounds rather literary. The words *because* and *since* seem to have taken its place.

He thought he had a good chance for a promotion, **for** his father was his manager's best friend.

Here are three examples of sentences being connected with coordinating conjunctions from the passage above:

A thrift store will sap your time, **but** it'll never sap your dinero.

Every thrifty diva I know has a fabulous thrift store find in her closet with a needle-in-a-haystack tale to tell, **but** you've got to be up for the hunt.

One easy way around this little caveat is to shop in a thin tee and skirt, **so** you can slip on tops and easily try on bottoms.

B. Use coordinating conjunctions

Combine each pair of sentences using coordinating conjunctions from the list above.

1.   I'm going shopping for shoes. I'm not going to spend more than one hundred dollars.

_____

2.   I studied algebra for five hours. I failed the test.

_____

3. The manager rejected my plans. I've got to change them.

   _____

4. He hung the clothes out to dry hours ago. They are still wet.

   _____

5. We can broil fish on the grill tonight. We can cook it in the oven.

   _____

6. The members complained loudly about the heat. They remained to give their opinions about the project.

   _____

VI.   READ IT AGAIN

Read the passage again. Answer the question.

Describe the kinds of clothes thrift stores sell.

_____

_____

SPIRITUALITY AND MEDITATION

I.   PRE-READING

A. Background information

Many of us have extremely busy lives. In our free time, we seek to get away from our hurried lifestyle. How can we do this without adding another time-consuming activity? In this excerpt, taken from the book *Save Your Brain: 5 Things You Must Do to Keep Your Mind Young and Sharp,* by Paul David Nussbaum, the author argues that spirituality and meditation offer great ways to relax.

B. Words to know before you read

Match the words to their definitions.

_____ 1. engagement

_____ 2. introspection

_____ 3. relaxation

_____ 4. chaotic

_____ 5. foster

_____ 6. generate

_____ 7. respite

_____ 8. addressing

a. a short period of time when you are able to stop doing something difficult

b. the act or state of being involved in something

c. an examination of one's own thoughts and feelings

d. time spent resting

e. to produce something

f. to help (something) grow or develop

g. giving specific attention to

h. state of confusion and disorder

C. Reading strategy

*This excerpt is about finding **balance** in your life. Circle the three words in the following sentences that have similar meanings to this idea of **balance**.*

Spirituality can help us to generate a more pleasing sense of balance and homeostasis (a stable state of equilibrium/mental or emotional balance).

Meditation can help you to slow down and turn inward for balance and symmetry.

II. READ

Read the excerpt. Mark the words you don't know, but don't stop reading to look them up.

Spirituality   When I talk about spirituality, I'm not necessarily addressing religion, but rather engagement in deep introspection or meditation as part of the human condition.

Spirituality has many meanings, and it may mean something different to you than me. This section refers to spirituality as one means of turning inward to foster a peaceful existence and to remove oneself from the hurried society. Sometimes spirituality takes the form of engaging in prayer, meditation, and other relaxation procedures.

Spirituality provides all of us techniques to slow down, turn inward, reduce the negative physiological effects of chronic stress on our brain and body, and help us to generate a more pleasing sense of balance and homeostasis (a stable state of equilibrium/mental or emotional balance). Consider these additional tips and ideas for you to express formal and informal spirituality in your daily life:

- Visit your favorite setting two to three times a week. This might be a community park, lake, beach, mountain base, river, or anywhere you feel at peace. Enjoy the beauty of your environment—taking in the beauty of your surrounding can also be considered spiritual.

- Get outside or simply remove your body and mind from the tasks that are in front of you. Everything else will be waiting for you when you return.

- Sometimes music helps when you retreat to your spiritual place. I like to download sounds of the ocean and waves and listen to soothing music while I pray or meditate.

Engaging in spirituality is a great way to stop, reflect, meditate, and relax to take a respite from our hurried lifestyle. While that is easily said and understood, it is also very difficult to change behavior. In order for you to achieve success with the spiritual domain as part of the brain health lifestyle, you must first identify stress in your life, where you experience stress in your body, and how you deal with stress now.

Meditation   Meditation can help you to slow down and turn inward for balance and symmetry. Your brain can adapt to a chaotic world, but it will function more efficiently over a longer period of time if you provide moments of inward reflection and rest. Meditation offers one technique to achieve such inner peace, and Western cultures are now more accepting of meditation and yoga.

Part of your brain health program can include a lesson or two on meditation so you can engage in this behavior on a daily basis. Fortunately, other cultures have already embraced the power of meditation and the benefits derived from deep introspection.

Source: *Save Your Brain: 5 Things You Must Do to Keep Your Mind Young and Sharp,* by Paul David Nussbaum, New York: McGraw-Hill, 2010

III. COMPREHENSION CHECK

Mark the sentences T (True) or F (False).

_____ 1. The author is talking about spirituality in religion.

_____ 2. The author is talking about spirituality as a way of turning inward to develop a peaceful existence.

_____ 3. Spirituality can take the form of prayer, meditation, or other forms of relaxation.

_____ 4. The author suggests you visit an amusement park to enjoy the beauty of the environment.

_____ 5. The author suggests you visit a lake or park to enjoy the beauty of the environment.

_____ 6. Engaging in spirituality is a way to take a break from a hurried lifestyle.

_____ 7. It is very easy to change behavior.

_____ 8. Your brain functions very efficiently in a chaotic world.

_____ 9. Meditation can help you slow down and give you balance.

_____ 10. In the last paragraph, the author is suggesting that you engage in meditation on a daily basis.

IV. VOCABULARY BUILDING

A. Understanding from context

Read the sentences. Before you look up words in the dictionary, use the context of each sentence to help you match the boldface words and idioms with the definitions that follow.

_____ 1. This section refers to spirituality as one means of **turning inward** to foster a peaceful existence and to remove oneself from the hurried society.

_____ 2. Meditation can help you to slow down and turn inward for balance and **symmetry**.

_____ 3. Your brain can adapt to a chaotic world, but it will function more **efficiently** over a longer period of time if you provide moments of inward reflection and rest.

_____ 4. **Fortunately**, other cultures have already embraced the power of meditation and the benefits derived from deep introspection.

_____ 5. Sometimes music helps when you **retreat** to your spiritual place.

_____ 6. While that is easily said and understood, it is also very difficult to change **behavior**.
   a. the ways you act
   b. go to a quiet place
   c. having good luck
   d. in the best way with the least waste of time and effort
   e. harmony and evenness among the parts of something
   f. shift attention from the outside world toward the mind or the self

B. Use the new words

Complete the sentences with the boldface words from Exercise A.

1. A human body has _____, with two arms, legs, and ears on both sides.

2. In school, the children have good _____ and generally don't goof around.

3. _____ and thinking deeply about my goals helps me stay focused.

4. If I work _____ I won't use all of my energy and time.

5. After a busy week, I just want to _____ to the seaside and relax.

6. _____, I brought enough warm clothes with me, as the weather was exceptionally cold.

V.   UNDERSTANDING GRAMMAR: ADVERBS OF OPINION

A. Read about adverbs of opinion

Adverbs of opinion express a speaker's viewpoint, opinion, or belief about an idea or situation.

Most adverbs of opinion can be placed at the beginning of a sentence, followed by a comma.

   Unfortunately, I failed my driver's test.

Adverbs of opinion may also be placed before a verb.

   I unfortunately failed my driver's test.

Here are twenty common adverbs of opinion ending in -ly:

fortunately	happily	honestly	
basically	luckily	undoubtedly	seriously
naturally	obviously	apparently	surprisingly
personally	strangely	surely	certainly
admittedly	surprisingly	clearly	assuredly

VI. READ IT AGAIN

Rewrite each sentence. Add the adverb of opinion.

1. She remembered to take her keys. [luckily]

   _____

2. We will be on time for the movie. [surely]

   _____

3. I will need to change some of my behaviors. [clearly]

   _____

4. He doesn't like to relax on the weekends. [strangely]

   _____

5. They don't like going to the mountains. [honestly]

   _____

6. I wouldn't recommend jogging at night. [personally]

   _____

7. She knows how to play several different instruments. [surprisingly]

   _____

8. We can't take a broken car on the trip. [obviously]

   _____

VII. READ IT AGAIN

Read the excerpt again. Answer the questions.

1. What are the benefits of spirituality?

   _____

   _____

2. What are the benefits of meditation?

   _____

   _____

SUCCESS AT SURFING

I. PRE-READING

A. Background information

This excerpt is taken from the book *Wingnut's Complete Surfing*, by Robert "Wingnut" Weaver. If you're near an ocean, surfing may just be the experience you need to get some exercise while getting in touch with nature. Surfing is a great pastime, not only in the United States, in places like California and Hawaii, but around the world as well.

B. Words to know before you read

Match the words to their definitions.

____ 1.	surfing	a.	becoming strong and healthier by exercising
____ 2.	sedentary	b.	not influenced or affected by something
____ 3.	immersed	c.	to cause someone to feel admiration
____ 4.	synthesis	d.	an award or expression of praise
____ 5.	conditioning	e.	something that is very popular for a period of time
____ 6.	prospective	f.	sport of riding ocean waves
____ 7.	immune	g.	to become smaller or less
____ 8.	malleable	h.	easily spread to other people
____ 9.	impress	i.	likely to happen in the future
____ 10.	accolades	j.	involving a lot of sitting
____ 11.	craze	k.	combination of different things
____ 12.	waned	l.	easily changed
____ 13.	infectious	m.	to take in or become engaged in completely

C. Reading strategy

Skim the article quickly, and write the answer to the question.

Why is surfing considered a "personal activity"?

_____

II. READ

Read the text. Mark the words you don't know, but don't stop reading to look them up.

Surfing Success

Can you remember, as a child, giving yourself wholly to the pursuit of an activity that brought you joy? It might have been swimming, shooting baskets, fishing, or some more sedentary activity, but while you were engaged in it hours would melt away unnoticed. When we come of age and in all likelihood are forced to spend an inordinate amount of time earning money, we forget the timeless joy of undistracted engagement in an activity pursued for its own sake. We forget how to play.

Surfing takes you back there. It makes you feel like a kid again. Even for the average, garden-variety participant, surfing is such a unique synthesis of physical exercise and conditioning, intellectual stimulation, and immersion in natural beauty, and is just so downright happy and thrilling, few who experience it can ever let it go. Surfing makes your soul smile.

Whether you start playing the guitar, taking golf lessons, training for marathons, acting, writing, learning martial arts, or participating on a sports team, you usually have an ultimate goal, conscious or unconscious, and you keep running and rerunning a cost-benefit analysis relative to that goal—prospective pain versus prospective gain. When will you consider yourself successful? When you receive an award, a trophy, or public acclaim?

Surfing is hardly immune from this sort of thinking, but success in surfing is fundamentally different. Maybe this is because of surfing's malleable, highly fluid nature and the fact that success is so completely defined by the participant. Surfing is an intensely personal activity—just you, your board, and a wave. Every day is different. All you have to do is catch the wave, stand up, ride, and do it again. . .three times, five times, ten times. You win. It doesn't matter whether you're surfing a one-foot wave on a sandy beach break or a roaring hollow monster at Pipeline on Oahu's famed North Shore. Many surfers continue into their seventies, a few into their nineties. It's the cheapest life insurance around. Success is measured purely by the personal happiness you generate. There is no obligation to impress others, win accolades, or even worry about what anyone else thinks.

This makes surfing about as close to pure fun as our species can approach on this particular planet. Other crazes come and go, yet the popularity of surfing has never waned since the modern worldwide explosion that began in the 1960s. There's a wave out there for everyone—every generation, race, and gender—and each surfer comes out a winner. Success in surfing is wrapped up in that infectious attitude of making every day great over the largest possible variety of conditions.

Source: *Wingnut's Complete Surfing*, by Robert "Wingnut" Weaver, New York: McGraw-Hill, 2009

III. COMPREHENSION CHECK

Mark the sentences T (True) or F (False).

_____ 1. When we become adults, we have to spend a lot of time making money, and we forget how to play.

_____ 2. Surfing makes you feel like a child again.

_____ 3. Surfing provides only intellectual stimulation.

_____ 4. Surfing makes you happy.

_____ 5. Usually when you take on an activity, you think only of the pain you will have to undergo.

_____ 6. Success in surfing is defined by each participant.

_____ 7. Every day, surfing stays the same and does not change.

_____ 8. People who surf the big waves, like a "roaring hollow monster" are the only winners.

_____ 9. People usually stop surfing when they turn fifty.

_____ 10. Success in surfing is measured by personal happiness.

_____ 11. To be successful in surfing, you must win awards and trophies.

_____ 12. In surfing, it's important to impress others.

_____ 13. Surfing became popular in the 1960s.

IV. VOCABULARY BUILDING

A. Understanding from context

Read the phrases. Before you look up words in the dictionary, use the context of each sentence to help you match the boldface words and idioms with the definitions that follow.

_____ 1. . . .**giving yourself wholly** to the pursuit of an activity that brought you joy. . .

_____ 2. It might have been swimming, **shooting baskets**, fishing. . .

_____ 3. . . .but while you were engaged in it hours would **melt away** unnoticed. . .

_____ 4. When we **come of age**. . .

_____ 5. . . .we forget the **timeless** joy. . .

_____ 6. Even for the average, **garden-variety** participant. . .

_____ 7. . . .a **cost-benefit analysis** relative to that goal. . .

_____ 8. . . .surfing's malleable, highly **fluid** nature. . .

_____ 9. There is no **obligation** to impress others. . .
   a. something that can change easily and often
   b. common/indistinguishable from a group
   c. a study of how much you have to pay for something, and what you will get in return
   d. to disappear
   e. reach adult status
   f. lasting forever
   g. something you must do
   h. to become fully engaged in something
   i. playing basketball

B. Use the new words

Complete the sentences with the boldface words and idioms from Exercise A.

1. The kids are _____ on the courts at the park.

2. She feels she has an _____ to be the best.

3. He's not a spectacular writer. He's just a _____ author.

4. They think their love is _____ and will never end.

5. Time seems to _____ when you're having fun.

6. You'll have many responsibilities when you _____.

7. If you are _____ to an activity, you are totally engaged.

8. Right now, we have a _____ situation that can change at any moment.

9. She performed a _____ to determine if she should spend time working on the project.

V. UNDERSTANDING GRAMMAR: PROPER NOUNS

A. Read about proper nouns.

There are two kinds of nouns: proper nouns and common nouns. Proper nouns are specific names of a person, place, thing, or idea. A common noun is the general name of a person or thing. Here are some examples:

common nouns	proper nouns
man	Fred
woman	Tinsae
country	Morocco
state	California

city	Addis Ababa
company	McGraw-Hill
store	Target
president	Barack Obama
river	Mississippi
school	Columbia University
restaurant	McDonald's

Note: Proper nouns are always capitalized.

B. Use the grammar

List two proper nouns from the passage.

_____   _____

In each blank, write a P if the boldface word is a proper noun and a C if the boldface word is a common noun.

1. _____ I visited my **cousins** last summer.

2. _____ She went skiing in **Colorado** this winter.

3. _____ I would like to go canoeing in the **river** soon.

4. _____ We bought a **Toyota** when our old car broke down.

5. _____ Her goal is to climb **Mt. Everest**.

6. _____ They're going to meet us at the **restaurant**.

7. _____ He'll attend school at **St. Paul's** next year.

VI.   READ IT AGAIN

Read the passage again. Answer the question.

How is success measured in surfing?

_____

BACKPACKING INTO THE WILDERNESS

I.   PRE-READING

A. Background information

This passage is from the *The Backpacker's Handbook*, by Chris Townsend. In this section of the introduction, Townsend talks about journeying into the wilderness to experience our natural world.

B. Words to know before you read

Match the words to their definitions.

____ 1. forgo   a. the highest point of a mountain

____ 2. invigorating   b. a wild or natural area where few people live

____ 3. odyssey   c. a steep rock or cliff

____ 4. mechanized   d. clean and germ-free

____ 5. sanitized   e. to cover in order to stop something from going in or out

____ 6. insulated   f. a strong material

____ 7. hiking   g. an area that is very dry, hot, and sandy

____ 8. wilderness   h. long journey full of adventures

____ 9. crag   i. walking a long distance for pleasure

____ 10. vista   j. flat area of land covered with tall grass

____ 11. desert   k. machinelike

____ 12. meadow   l. a large and beautiful view of an area of land or water

____ 13. nylon   m. to give up the use of or enjoyment of

____ 14. summit   n. lively

C. Reading strategy

This passage contains many nature words. Quickly read through the text, and underline all of the words relating to nature.

II. READ

Read the text. Mark the words you don't know, but don't stop reading to look them up.

Why backpack? Why forgo the comforts of home or hotel for a night under the stars or sheltered by a flimsy nylon sheet? Many people hike in the wilds but return to civilization at night. This is experiencing only part of what the wilderness has to offer; it's like dipping your toe in the water instead of taking an invigorating swim. Only by living in the wilderness twenty-four hours a day, day after day, do you gain that indefinable feeling of rightness, of being with instead of against the earth, that gives the deepest contentment I have found.

The heart of backpacking lies in the concept of the journey itself, a true odyssey, a desire to explore a world beyond our everyday lives, and in doing so to explore ourselves. Not so long ago, all journeys were like this, because the known world extended little beyond one's hometown. Now, with modern communications and mass transportation, most "journeys" consist of nothing more than the mechanized moving of bodies from one place to another, a process so sanitized, safe, controlled, and so insulated from its surroundings that it precludes any sense of freedom, adventure, or personal involvement. Only when I shoulder my pack and set out into the wilderness do I feel a journey is really beginning, even though I may have traveled halfway around the world to take that first step.

Though being in the wilderness is what matters, and the real goal of any hike is to experience nature, a more specific purpose gives shape to a trip and provides an incentive to keep moving. Thus I always set a goal, even on day hikes—a summit, a lake, a distance to cover, a crag to visit, a vista to see. Once I'm under way, the overall goal is subordinated to the day-by-day, minute-by-minute events and impressions that are my reason for hiking.

Walking is the only way to really see a place, to really grasp what it's like, to experience all its aspects. This is true even for cities but applies much, much more to mountains and deserts, forests and meadows. Seen from a car, a train, or even a "scenic viewpoint," these are only pretty pictures, postcard images for the surface of the mind, quickly forgotten. By walking through a landscape, you enter into it, experience it with every one of your senses, learn how it works and why it's as it is. You become, for a time, a part of it. And once you stay out overnight and entrust your sleeping self to its care, a deeper bond is forged and, fleetingly and at the edge of your mind, you begin to grasp that we are not *apart* from but *part* of the earth.

This process of exploring the relationship between the self and the natural world grows and expands as you become more experienced and confident in wilderness wandering. It does not, I suspect, have limits.

By experiencing the wilderness directly, by being in touch with the land, we can learn how valuable—how essential—it is, and that we must try to preserve and restore our still-beautiful world.

Source: *The Backpacker's Handbook,* by Chris Townsend, New York: McGraw-Hill, 1949

III. COMPREHENSION CHECK

Choose the correct completion for each sentence.

1. The main idea of this passage is:

   a. backpacking through the wilderness gives you a chance to live apart from nature.

   b. backpacking through the wilderness gives you a chance to experience nature, have a closer relationship with the earth, and realize how you are a part of it.

   c. backpacking through the wilderness shows you how important good boots are.

2. In backpacking, the journey is important because it gives us the opportunity to

    a. use modern communication.

    b. explore our hometown.

    c. explore a world beyond our everyday lives.

3. Modern communication and transportation have made traveling

    a. safe and controlled.

    b. adventurous.

    c. an exploration.

4. The goal of any hike should be

    a. returning to civilization.

    b. experiencing modern transportation.

    c. being in the wilderness.

5. _____ is the way to "really see a place" and "really grasp what it's like."

    a. Looking at a postcard

    b. Walking

    c. Driving

6. By exploring the wilderness, we learn that our land is valuable, and that we must try to

    a. use more natural resources.

    b. preserve and restore it.

    c. build more houses on it.

IV. VOCABULARY BUILDING

A. Identify meaning

Choose the words that have the same meaning as the underlined words.

1. The paper plates are too <u>flimsy</u> to hold a lot of food.

    a. weak

    b. strong

    c. old

2. We <u>subordinated</u> our desire to eat in order to continue playing the game.

    a. raised

    b. lowered

    c. interrupted

3. My best friend and I tell each other everything; we have a very strong <u>bond</u>.

    a. connection

    b. separation

    c. fascination

4. We <u>forged</u> a friendship when we were in the second grade.

    a. broke

    b. destroyed

    c. formed

5. My fears of the wilderness were <u>fleeting</u>, and I quickly became comfortable sleeping under the stars.

    a. short-lived

    b. slowly

    c. strong

6. It is <u>essential</u> to drink water if you are exercising.

    a. extremely difficult

    b. extremely important

    c. extremely dangerous

7. The cookies were good <u>incentives</u> for getting the children to work faster.

    a. feelings

    b. tests

    c. motivators

8. The beauty of the mountains left a strong <u>impression</u> in my mind.

    a. mental picture

    b. mental turmoil

    c. mental block

B. Idioms

The idiom *to be in touch with* has several different meanings. Here are two examples:

having a deep understanding and appreciation of something

> *She's really **in touch with** animals and can tell when they are depressed.*

being in communication with someone

> *Are you **in touch with** your friends from college, or have you grown apart?*

Copy the sentence from the text that uses this idiom.

_____

_____

V. UNDERSTANDING GRAMMAR: PREFIXES *IN-*, *RE-*, AND *PRE-*

A. Read about prefixes *in-*, *re-*, and *pre-*.

A prefix is a group of letters that can be added to the beginning of a word or a "root word" to change the meaning of the word.

A root word is a word that can stand on its own. You can make a new word from it by adding a prefix to the beginning of it.

B. The meaning of prefixes

Every prefix has a meaning. For example:

Prefix	Meaning	Examples
in-	into, toward, not	<u>instead</u>: *in* = "in" + *stead* = "standing" definition: in place of; as a substitute <u>indefinable</u>: *in* = "not" + *definable* = "to explain the meaning of" <u>invigorate</u>: (from Latin) *in* = "toward" + *vigorare* = "make strong" definition: to fill with life or energy
re-	again, back	<u>return</u>: (from Latin) *re* = "back" + *tourner* = "to turn" definition: to go or come back to a place again <u>restore</u>: (from Latin) *restaurare* = "to renew" definition: to return something to an earlier or original condition
pre-	before	<u>preclude</u>: (from Latin) *prae* = before + *claudere* = to close definition: to make something impossible or prevent something from happening <u>preserve</u>: (from Latin) *prae* = before + *servāre* = to keep safe definition: to keep safe or keep alive

Knowing the meaning of a prefix can help you to determine the meaning of the word.

C. Use the grammar

Write the correct prefix word in each blank. Use the correct verb form.

indiscreet	prearrange	repaint
infertile	preheat	reassemble
inappropriate	precede	inactive
pregame	renew	

1. We attended a _____ party before the final game.

2. An _____ person would tell all of your secrets to everyone.

3. Nothing will grow in _____ soil.

4. She will _____ the seating of the guests before the dinner.

5. If you know you will not be finished reading a book before it is due back to the library, you may want to _____ it.

6. Before putting a cake in the oven to bake, you need to _____ the oven.

7. Wearing a sports jersey to a fine restaurant is _____.

8. If the paint on your house is chipped or has changed colors in places due to the harsh weather, you may want to _____ it.

9. She closed all of the accounts that were _____.

10. We could not _____ the toy because it had been broken into too many parts.

11. The president that _____ the current one was not very effective.

VI. READ IT AGAIN

Read the passage again. Answer the question.

What are the benefits of "walking through a landscape" and spending the night under the stars?

_____

_____

_____

Answer Key

1. NATURE IN THE UNITED STATES

Yellowstone Park rules

I-B 1. e 2. g 3. f 4. c 5. a 6. b 7. d

I-C 10

III 1. F 2. T 3. F 4. T 5. T 6. T 7. F 8. T 9. T 10. F

IV-A 1. i 2. a 3. c 4. d 5. h 6. b 7. f 8. j 9. g 10. e

IV-B 1. defacing 2. obtain 3. restrictions 4. valid 5. Feel free 6. designated
7. display 8. thoroughly 9. Keep in mind 10. unattended

IV-C Adjectives: wearable, archeological, slow-moving, unwelcome, thermal.
Nouns: routes, boardwalks, trails, flotation device, pullouts, fire grates, chain saws

IV-D 1. unwelcome 2. wearable 3. archeological 4. slow-moving
5. thermal 6. trails 7. routes 8. chain saw 9. boardwalks
10. flotation device 11. pullout 12. fire grate

V-B 1. established, Active 2. was established, Passive 3. can be found, Passive
4. can find, Active 5. may see, Active 6. may be seen, Passive
7. must not take, Active 8. must not be taken, Passive

VI 1. The following activities are completely prohibited: disturbing park features
(possessing, collecting, removing, defacing, or destroying any natural or archeological
objects or plants, animals, or minerals); feeding wildlife; using chain saws; leaving
food unattended; littering; leaving a pet unattended or tied to an object.

2. The following activities are restricted: bicycling, boating, climbing, driving,
lighting fires, bringing pets.

Grand Canyon National Park

I-B 1. d 2. f 3. e 4. c 5. a 6. g 7. b

I-C 8,000

III 1. 5 million 2. spring, summer, and fall 3. winter weather 4. South Rim
5. mid-May through mid-October 6. five hours 7. Walking at such elevation
can be strenuous.

IV 1a. crowded 1b. crowd 2a. reserve 2b. reservation 2c. reserved
3a. congested 3b. congestion 4a. consider 4b. considerate 4c. consideration
5a. access 5b. accessible 5c. access 6a. identify 6b. identifiable
6c. identification 7a. difficulty 7b. difficult

V 1. less 2. fewer 3. fewer 4. less 5. fewer

VI 1. The Grand Canyon has an average of five million visitors annually and is
crowded most of the year

2. The North Rim is less crowded, but it has fewer facilities, is less accessible, and
is only open mid-May through mid-October

Saving trees

I-B   1. f   2. e   3. a   4. b   5. c   6. d

I-C   More than three thousand years old

III   1. a   2. b   3. b   4. b   5. b

IV-B   1. blizzard   2. drought   3. flood   4. disease   5. avalanche   6. mudslide

V-B   1. It takes five hours to drive from Las Vegas to the Grand Canyon.   2. It is a 25-mile hike from the South Rim to the North Rim.   3. It takes 17 days to raft through the Grand Canyon on the Colorado River.   4. It took nine years for Muir and others to stop the logging in Sequoia National Park.   5. It took Reinhold Metzger six days to backpack the 211-mile John Muir trail.

VI   1. loggers   2. To compare and connect humans with the Sequoias

An outdoor survival school

I-B   1. c   2. a   3. d   4. f   5. b   6. e

I-C   1. So hungry he could eat a squirrel   2. 36 degrees

II   1. T   2. F   3. F   4. T   5. T   6. T   7. T   8. T   9. F   10. T

III-A   1. prickly   2. rusty   3. sooty   4. ravenous   5. laborious   6. bloodshot
7. soaring

III-B   1. feed   2. billowed   3. roast   4. enclosed   5. shell   6. stuck   7. froze
8. boiled   9. collected

IV-B   1. Despite the rain, we went for a hike.   2. Despite the difficulty, we finished the project. Despite the congestion, the city was beautiful.

V   1. Collecting onions and acorns   2. They fed the fire.

Excerpt from Hatchet by Gary Paulson

I-B   1. e   2. f   3. b   4. d   5. a   6. c

I-C   hit him, threw him into the water, and drove him down into the bottom

III   1. b   2. b   3. a   4. b   5. a   6. a

IV-A   tiger: fur, paws, claws, tail, whiskers; salmon: gills, scales, fin; hawk: claws, beak, feather; bison: horns, fur, tail, hooves

IV-B   1. tiger   2. hawk   3. bison   4. salmon

V   1. darker and darker   2. hungrier and hungrier   3. easier and easier
4. more and more frustrated   5. thinner and thinner

VI   1. Something caught his ear or his nose.   2. The moose drove him into the muck then left.

2. THE 20TH CENTURY

Technology time line

I-B   1. d   2. e   3. a   4. f   5. c   6. b

I-C   The first space shuttle went up.; PCs became popular.

III   1. F   2. F   3. T   4. T   5. T   6. T

IV-A   1. d   2. b   3. a   4. e   5. c

IV-B 1. NASA's Apollo 11 spacecraft 2. Neil Armstrong 3. Bill Gates
4. personal computers 5. genetic engineering

IV-C 1. witnessed 2. launches 3. retrieve 4. alter 5. vowed 6. dominate
7. seeking 8. implant

V-B 1. Tim Berners-Lee creates the World Wide Web. 2. The DVD is
invented. 3. Apple Computer announces the release of the iPod. 4. Toyota
produces its first hybrid car. 5. Time Magazine names YouTube the invention of
the year. 6. For the first time, people in the United States send more text
messages than they make phone calls. 7. Movies in 3-D become the rage.
8. The Apple iPad comes out and sells millions of units.

VI Artificial heart

Bill Gates at college

I-C The Altair 8080

III 1. T 2. F 3. T 4. F 5. T

IV 1. gave the impression 2. hackers 3. race 4. dorm 5. nerd 6. instead of
7. bright 8. dandruff 9. rival 10. spotted 11. not amount to anything

V-B 1. was studying 2. were attending 3. were trying 4. was becoming

VI It was his opportunity to do something with BASIC.

Rock against the Berlin Wall

I-C David Bowie, the Eurythmics, and Genesis

III 1. Berlin City Hall 2. summer 3. three nights 4. chase away the
crowd 5. everyone below the age of 30

IV-A 1a. chased 1b. chase 2a. blast 2b. blasting 3a. clustered 3b. cluster
4a. chants 4b. chanted 5a. arrests 5b. arrested

IV-B 1. set up 2. turned out 3. let on 4. set off

V-B 1. After there were food shortages in many cities, people began to
protest. 2. After the wall was torn down in 1989, people began collecting pieces
of it. 3. After the wall opened up East Berlin, many rock groups had concerts to
celebrate. 4. After the Berliners tore down the wall on November 9, people from
all over came to the site to celebrate.

VI It was the first of the East German protests of the 1980s that played a part in
bringing down the wall.

JFK's inaugural speech

I-B 1. d 2. a 3. e 4. c 5. f 6. b

I-C President Kennedy is calling on the world as a whole to work together to
overcome the problems that all humans face, across all nations.

III 1. Tyranny, poverty, disease, and war itself 2. North and South, East and
West (the entire world) 3. The responsibility to defend freedom 4. Ask what
they can do for their country 5. Ask what they can do with the United States for
the freedom of man

IV-A   1. forge   2. alliance   3. more fruitful   4. granted, defend   5. shrink
6. devotion, endeavor   7. glow

IV-B   1. alliance   2. glow   3. assured   4. poverty   5. granted   6. devotion
7. disease   8. endeavor

V-C   1. I don't know if we can win this struggle.   2. I'd like to know if he can
assure them that they'll be safe.   3. I'm not sure if we can benefit from this
endeavor.   4. I wonder if they can see the glow from the fireplace.   5. Do you
know why they can't form an alliance?

VI   Overcoming tyranny, poverty, disease, and war

Facing tanks in North Africa

I-B   1. c   2. f   3. e   4. b   5. a   6. d

I-C   Four

III   1. T   2. F   3. F   4. T   5. F   6. F

IV-A   1. f   2. a   3. c   4. e   5. h   6. d   7. g   8. b

IV-B   1. gripped   2. staggered   3. seeking   4. ripped   5. wounded
6. shattered   7. scrambled   8. jerked

V-B   1. The soldiers were seeking a safe place to enter.   2. The commander knew
his men would quickly obey.   3. The gunfire was shattering the door into a
thousand pieces.   4. He was calling orders as he went.   5. One soldier was
driving the tank while another was using the machine gun.

VI   1. There was smoke in the tank.   2. Because of the smoke, the fighting all
around them, the shattering blast, the tank, the enemy only yards away, and the
confusion

3. SAN FRANCISCO

City travel tips

I-B   1. c   2. f   3. d   4. b   5. a   6. e

I-C   what to wear, the weather, going to restaurants, interesting places to visit,
public transportation, making conversation, parking

III   1. F   2. T   3. T   4. T   5. F   6. F   7. T   8. T   9. T   10. F

IV-A   1. c   2. e   3. a   4. f   5. g   6. h   7. d   8. b

IV-B   1. steep   2. pedal   3. thereabouts   4. herd   5. Hailing   6. newsworthy
7. regret   8. paddle

IV-C   1. unforgettable   2. quirky   3. local   4. steep   5. local   6. unforgettable
7. quirky   8. steep

V-D   1. If you go to San Francisco, be sure to visit Golden Gate Park.   2. N/A
3. If you want to visit nearby cities, you can take a ferry or BART.   4. If you have
children, you should visit the Exploratorium.   5. N/A

V-E   1. visit   2. will see   3. rains   4. will need   5. ask

VI   1. Do not bring your parka and ski gloves; do not go to the Civic Center
after dark; do not assume the ticket you bought for BART works on MUNI; do
not call the city "Frisco" or "San Fran."   2. Parking is near impossible; you can
rent a bike; the public transportation is rather good.

A guide to city neighborhoods

I-B 1. d 2. g 3. h 4. f 5. b 6. a 7. c 8. e

I-C Grant Street: the oldest street in San Francisco; Lombard Street: sinuous curves of the street; Mission Dolores: the oldest structure in San Francisco

III 1. Grant Avenue and Bush Street 2. exotic shops, food markets, temples, and small museums 3. Notre Dame in Paris 4. Russian hunters who were active in California waters in the early 1800s 5. Some of the best weather in the city with an abundance of fog-free days 6. New restaurants and nightspots

IV-A 1. noun 2. verb 3. verb 4. adjective 5. verb 6. verb 7. noun 8. noun 9. adjective 10. noun 11. adjective 12. adjective

IV-B verbs: 1. comprises 2. boasted 3. took place 4. took advantage of adjectives: 5. sinuous 6. adjacent 7. exotic 8. noble nouns: 9. replica 10. hunter 11. abundance 12. remedy

V-B 1. tallest 2. longest 3. busiest 4. most expensive 5. steepest 6. largest

VI Examples: Chinatown's Grant Avenue is the oldest street in San Francisco.; Nob Hill includes Russian Hill, which is most famous for the sinuous curves of Lombard Street.; The Mission District has the best weather.

A new gold rush

I-B 1. c 2. f 3. b 4. e 5. a 6. d

I-C 1. A piece of equipment used to sift for gold. 2. A deep red gemstone.

III 1. F 2. F 3. F 4. T 5. T 6. T

IV-A 1. a 2. b 3. a 4. b 5. b 6. a 7. a 8. b.

IV-B 1. strike it rich 2. promising 3. rushing 4. illusions 5. hopped 6. hiked 7. jutting out 8. refined

IV-C hiked, hopped, looked, shoveled, sifted, sorted, deposited

V-B 1. PT 2. ST 3. C 4. ST 5. C 6. PT

VI 1. Mike Gavin is a Los Alamitos roofer, and Mark Montelius is a self-employed handyman. 2. The sluicer is placed into the river to let water run through it as it catches the heaviest particles in its carpetlike bottom.

Caught up in the 1906 earthquake

I-B 1. c 2. a 3. b 4. e 5. f 6. d

I-C The tenement house collapsed, and Mrs. Whitlaw's fence toppled over.

III 1. b 2. a 3. b 4. a 5. b

IV-A 1. debris 2. collapse 3. immense 4. mound 5. twists 6. shuddered 7. collapsed 8. twisted 9. mounds 10. immense 11. debris 12. shudder

V-B 1. had moved 2. had fallen 3. had gotten hurt 4. had broken

V-C 1. had woken up, hit 2. realized, had not prepared 3. destroyed, had not fallen 4. went, had collapsed 5. remembered, had shuddered

VI 1. Metal, bricks, wood, and wood nails 2. Tearing, crashing, breaking free, cracking, tinkling

The development of Alcatraz

I-B 1. g 2. e 3. d 4. f 5. b 6. a 7. c

I-C 1848, 1853, 1861, 1898, 1906, 1912, the late 1920s

III 1848, the late 1920s, 1898, 1853, 1906, 1912, 1861

IV 1a. catastrophe 1b. catastrophic 2a. confined 2b. confinement
2c. confined 3a. abundant 3b. abundance 4a. seized 4b. seizure 5a. resource
5b. resourceful 6a. hazardous 6b. hazard 7a. isolated 7b. Isolation 7c. isolate

V-B 1. would be 2. would hit 3. were confined 4. would close

VI 1. Alcatraz was a good place for a prison because of its natural isolation.
2. The Civil War and the Spanish-American War

4. THE EARLY UNITED STATES

Civil War reenactment

I-B 1. b 2. e 3. d 4. f 5. c 6. g 7. a

I-C 1. A York County field 2. Saturday 3. 2 P.M.

III 1. Battle of Huck's Defeat 2. A collection of homes, farm buildings, and
gardens about 35 miles southwest of Charlotte 3. 18 4. Red wool vests and
canvas leggings 5. It feels like he's going back in time.

IV-A 1. The sound of musket fire 2. Dennis Marcone 3. Shorts and
t-shirts 4. History is the subject his father taught. 5. 1780 6. Historic
Brattonsville 7. Shots rang out from the woods near a house surrounded by
British soldiers.

IV-B 1. looked on 2. got hooked on 3. got under way 4. found out
5. takes me back 6. turned the tide

V-B 1. As 2. as if 3. as if 4. as 5. as 6. as if

VI The Battle of Huck's Defeat turned the tide of the war.

"Paul Revere's Ride"

I-B Hang a light up high in the bell tower of the North Church tower to give
information

I-C 3-4—Seventy-five/alive

6-8—march/arch

7-9—to-night/light

10-11—sea/be

12-13-14—alarm/farm/arm

110-111—read/fled

112-113—ball/wall

114-115—lane/again

116-117—road/load

118-121—Revere/fear

119-120—alarm/farm

122-123—door/evermore

III 1. April 18, 1775 2. Two 3. Arm themselves 4. Behind fences and farmyard walls

IV 1. b 2. a 3. a 4. a 5. a 6. a 7. b 8. b

V 1. We hardly ever go to the movies. 2. He had hardly loaded the gun when he had to fire. 3. He had hardly closed the book when he fell asleep. 4. There were hardly any professional soldiers in the army. 5. They hardly ever spoke about the problem.

VI 1. The Regulars and the Redcoats 2. This was the beginning of the American Revolution.

The Declaration of Independence

I-B 1. g 2. d 3. h 4. e 5. a 6. b 7. f 8. c

I-C Creator, Rights, Life, Liberty, Happiness, Governments, Men, Form, Government, Right, People, Government, Safety, Happiness

III 1. a 2. b 3. a 4. b 5. a

IV-B 1a. alterations 1b. altered 2a. created 2b. creations 2c. creator 3a. destroyed 3b. destruction 3c. destructive 4a. equal 4b. equality 5a. evidence 5b. evident 6a. happy 6b. happiness 7a. institute 7b. institution 8a. safety 8b. safe

V-A 1. thought, believed 2. believe, realize 3. learned, discovered 4. believed, thought, decided 5. hoped, assumed, believed, thought, knew

VI Life, liberty, and the pursuit of happiness

Christopher Columbus' Journal

I-C 1. They came to the ship in canoes. 2. Columbus learned that there was a king southward around the island who possessed large vessels of gold, and in great quantities.

III 1. c 2. a 3. b 4. c 5. c

IV-A

verb	noun
row	canoe
empty	oar
steer	cotton
right	parrot
gather	trunk
upset	quantity

IV-B 1. oar 2. parrots 3. upset 4. steered 5. gathered 6. trunk 7. empty 8. right 9. row 10. canoe 11. cotton 12. quantity

V-B 1. They traded with the visitors until the visitors left. 2. He explored the Caribbean until it was time to go home. 3. They worked on the building until midnight. 4. They continued searching for gold in the New World until they died.

VI Whatever Columbus gave them.

5. ENTERTAINMENT

The main movie genres

I-B 1. f 2. e 3. g 4. c 5. d 6. a 7. h 8. b

I-C Action, drama, horror, sci-fi

III 1. T 2. T 3. F 4. F 5. F 6. T 7. F 8. T 9. T 10. F 11. T 12. T

IV-A

nouns	verbs	adjectives
crises	captivate	deranged
range	overlap	improbable
rhythm		
havoc		

IV-B 1. havoc 2. deranged 3. improbable 4. range 5. crises 6. captivate
7. rhythm 8. overlap

V-B 1. This old house is really livable. 2. They told the hero that the mountain was not climbable. 3. Some small dogs are very excitable. 4. That point is debatable. 5. She likes to buy microwavable popcorn. 6. When he cut his hair and grew a beard, he was not recognizable.

VI 1. Action and sci-fi 2. They are serious and plot-driven, portraying realistic characters, settings, life situations, and stories involving intense character development and interaction. Usually, they are not focused on special effects, comedy, or action.

Reviews for Titanic

I-B 1. d 2. e 3. f 4. g 5. b 6. c 7. a

I-C c. (Howe)

III 1. T 2. F 3. T 4. T 5. F 6. T

IV-A 1a. romance 1b. romantic 2a. traditional 2b. tradition
3a. extravagance 3b. extravagant 4a. exhilaration 4b. exhilarating
5a. flaws 5b. flawless 6a. poems 6b. poetic 7a. intelligent 7b. intelligence

IV-B 1. b 2. c 3. a

V-B 1. The young man said hello cheerfully. 2. The owners inspected the ship closely. 3. The older man spoke to the young woman kindly. 4. The story was sadly told by the old woman. 5. The ship was faithfully reproduced by the director. 6. The movie did not end happily.

VI 1. Spellbinding, exhilarating, stunning 2. Technology astounds, the physical spectacle

From Norma Jeane to Marilyn Monroe

I-B 1. c 2. e 3. f 4. a 5. b 6. d

I-C 1. 1944, 1945 2. World War II

III   1. 1944   2. A defense factory   3. David Conover   4. 19   5. The Blue Book Modeling Agency   6. Twentieth Century-Fox   7. Yes

IV-A   put off, look back, in turn, put in touch with, pass on

IV-B   1. looks back on   2. passed on   3. put off   4. put in touch with   5. in turn

IV-D   1. landed   2. posed   3. intervened   4. joined   5. spotted

V-B   1. He took on an extra job to earn more money.   2. She worked day and night to be successful.   3. She joined an acting class to improve her skill.
4. She put off having children to focus on her career.   5. She acted in commercials and in small TV roles to gain experience.

VI   When her husband left for the war, she began to work at a defense factory where David Conover photographed her. Conover gave the photos to a booking agency, starting her modeling career and leading to her film career.

All the world's a stage

I- C   The infant, the whining school boy, the lover, second childhood

III   1. b   2. a   3. b   4. a   5. a   6. b

IV-A   1. d   2. b   3. g   4. f   5. c   6. a   7. h   8. e

IV-B   1. whining   2. furnace   3. stage   4. shining   5. merely   6. unwilling
7. creeping   8. eventful

V-B   1. paying   2. sleeping   3. singing   4. captivating   5. acting

VI   *Infant:* mewling, puking; *schoolboy:* creeping, unwilling; *lover:* sighing, woeful; *last:* oblivion

6. EATING IN, EATING OUT
Restaurant reviews

I-B   1. b   2. e   3. a   4. f   5. c   6. d

I-C   Three

III   1. d   2. a   3. e   4. b   5. c

IV-A   1. Freda's   2. Freda's   3. Freda's   4. Carmelo's Italian Restaurant
5. Carmelo's Italian Restaurant   6. Carmelo's Italian Restaurant   7. Rivals
Steakhouse   8. Truluck's Austin Arboretum   9. Truluck's Austin Arboretum
10. County Line on the Hill   11. County Line on the Hill

IV-B   1. b   2. a   3. c   4. c   5. b   6. b   7. a   8. b   9. b   10. a   11. b

V-B   1. was terrible   2. warm   3. listen to loud music   4. the server didn't take our order   5. wave our hands   6. looking   7. fresh crab   8. left

VI   1. locally owned, upscale yet casual   2. located downtown, offers complimentary valet parking   3. stylish comfortable environment   4. own fisheries in Naples, Florida, have an outdoor patio   5. located in the Texas Hill Country, offer outdoor seating with a stellar view

Choices on a Denny's menu

I-B

vegetable (or plant)	meat or seafood	other
spinach	bacon	caramel
garlic	sausage	dressing
pickle	prime rib	pasta
herb	chicken breast	sauce
cucumber	meatball	toast
mushroom	shrimp	gravy
celery	pot roast	

I-C   six

III   1. Peppers, onions, spinach, mushrooms, and tomatoes   2. Banana   3. 11 A.M.
to 10 P.M.   4. Mushrooms and onions   5. Melted swiss cheese and mushrooms
sautéed in garlic and herbs   6. Golden-fried breaded chicken strips or a grilled
seasoned chicken breast   7. A rich, meaty tomato sauce   8. Grilled shrimp
skewer or six golden-fried shrimp   9. Rich gravy

IV-B   1. kettle-cooked   2. fire-roasted   3. herb-roasted   4. sautéed
5. grilled or fried   6. shredded   7. fried or grilled

IV-C   1. fried   2. grilled   3. melted   4. sautéed   5. fire-roasted

V-B   1. frying   2. serve   3. sauté   4. fried   5. roasting   6. serving   7. roasted
8. sautéed

VI   1. five   2. Dinner

Trends in supermarket foods

I-B   1. c   2. e   3. d   4. b   5. f   6. a

I-C   Vegetables, fruits, produce, jicama, choyote, bok choy, daikon radishes,
asparagus, butter, lemon, hollandaise, rosemary, garlic, spears, Thai peanut sauce

III   1. b   2. a   3. c

IV-B   1. carry   2. course   3. waves   4. just   5. carry   6. produce   7. waves,
waves   8. carry   9. produce   10. stocks   11. waves   12. just   13. stocks

IV-C   We have the world and its flavors at our fingertips.

V-B   1. I didn't have much money, even though I bought an expensive dinner.
2. I buy that vegetable because it's healthy, although I don't really like it.
3. I don't usually like cabbage, though I love bok choy.   4. The market carries a
lot of Latin American produce, though they don't stock jicama.   5. We don't have
access to a wide variety of fruits, although it is possible to find unusual vegetables.

VI   Asia and Latin America

Hunting for dinner

I-B   1. d   2. e   3. a   4. b   5. c

I-C   Angelo

III   1. T   2. F   3. T   4. F   5. F

IV-A 1. parade 2. clearing 3. steep 4. excruciating 5. squeeze
6. summon 7. flank 8. self-restraint

V-B 1. They, roasting 2. She, breathing 3. He, describing

V-C 1. We bought the dinner, paying for the meal, the drinks, and the tip.
2. She worked on a modern small-scale farm, raising chickens and growing
organic vegetables. 3. She took care of the chicken, allowing them to wander
free and eat insects. 4. They walked through the forest, moving slowly and
listening for the sounds of the animals.

VI lightly, self-restraint, excruciatingly slow

Christmas morning breakfast

I-B 1. d 2. g 3. f 4. b 5. c 6. a 7. e

I-C Jo, Beth, Amy, Meg

III 1. F 2. F 3. T 4. F 5. T 6. T 7. F 8. F

IV-A 1. heroically 2. eager 3. impetuous 4. impetuously 5. eagerly
6. heroic

IV-B 1. make up 2. exclaimed 3. huddled 4. kept on 5. suffering 6. piled

V-B 1. could/can 2. May 3. Could/Can 4. Could/Can 5. May

VI Mrs. March is satisfied because her daughters are willing to give up their
Christmas breakfast for their poor neighbors.

7. PLAYING THE GAME

The rules for checkers

I-B 1. d 2. g 3. b 4. e 5. f 6. d 7. a

I-C 1. 12 2. 64

III 1. F 2. T 3. F 4. T

IV-A 1. a 2. b 3. b 4. b 5. a 6. a 7. b 8. b 9. a 10. b 11. b

IV-B 1. diagonally 2. opposing 3. typically 4. alternate 5. typical
6. diagonally 7. opponent 8. alternating 9. shifting 10. opposed 11. shifted

V-B 1. so 2. so that 3. so 4. so 5. so that 6. so 7. so that 8. so

VI So the piece is crowned and becomes king

"Take Me Out to the Ball Game"

I-B 1. c 2. e 3. f 4. b 5. a 6. d Baseball words: 1. b 2. a

I-C baseball

III 1. F 2. T 3. T 4. T 5. F

IV-A 1. f 2. c 3. b 4. d 5. a 6. e

IV-B 1. fever 2. cheer up 3. gang 4. get back 5. blow 6. score

V-B 1. d 2. b 3. a 4. f 5. c 6. e

V-C 1. b 2. b 3. b 4. a 5. b

VI Direct speech: Miss Kate said "No, I'll tell you what you can do"; Reported
speech: Told the umpire he was wrong

The attraction of golf

I-B   1. f   2. e   3. g   4. a   5. b   6. c   7. d

I-C   1. Arnold Palmer and Jack Nicklaus   2. two of the greatest golfers of our time

III   1. T   2. F   3. T

IV-A   1. b   2. a   3. b   4. a   5. b   6. a   7. a

IV-B   1. enhances   2. solitude   3. endured   4. affords   5. appeal   6. execute   7. lure

V-B   1. subject: top athletes; prepositional phrase: in major sports; verb: make   2. subject: book; prepositional phrase: about his experiences growing up; verb: was   3. subject: Driving; prepositional phrase: under the influence of alcohol; verb: is   4. subject: Several of the restaurants; prepositional phrase: around town; verbs: are offering   5. subject: lines; prepositional phrase: on his forehead; verbs: deepened, got   6. subject: The witness's explanation; prepositional phrase: of the events; verbs: didn't make

VI   For the feeling of solitude and self-reliance that affords him supreme independence

The invention of basketball

I-B   1. f   2. d   3. g   4. a   5. b   6. c   7. e

I-C   A member of the gym class, a Southerner from North Carolina, a tackle on the football team, and a leader of the group of students

III   1. He tacked the rules to a bulletin board.   2. He was sure in his own mind that the game was good.   3. Frank Mahan was the ringleader of the group, and if he did not approve of the new game, no one in the class would. They had also tried numerous other new games that were apparently unsuccessful.   4. He promised them that if the new game was a failure, he would not try any more experiments.   5. Yes the game was a success.

IV-A   1. e   2. f   3. a   4. c   5. b   6. d

IV-B   1. instant   2. made her way   3. gazed   4. proceeded to   5. failure   6. fastened

V-B   1. then/and then   2. Then   3. then/and then   4. then   5. then/and then

VI   The basketball game was the end of the trouble with the class because they all enjoyed it and the teacher succeeded.

Toward the finishing line

I-B   1. b   2. d   3. e   4. c   5. a   Horse-racing words: 1. c   2. a   3. b

I-C   North Face; yes

III   1. T   2. T   3. F

IV-A   1. d   2. c   3. g   4. h   5. b   6. a   7. e   8. f

IV-B   1. rejected   2. urged   3. accelerates   4. dimly   5. drastically   6. wavers   7. resistance   8. incline

V-B   1. adjective: black; noun: coffee   2. adjective: green; noun: house   3. adjective: happy; noun: her   4. adjective: useless; noun: machine

5. adjective: difficult; noun: work   6. adjective: awake; noun: me

V-C   1. cold   2. yellow   3. interested   4. exciting   5. angry   6. finished

VI   The jockey thought he was winning so he half dropped his hands.

8. SICKNESS AND HEALTH

Rules for healthful eating

I-B   1. b   2. f   3. e   4. a   5. h   6. d   7. c   8. g   9. k   10. i   11. j

I-C   1. Eat fresh foods.   2. Plan your meals and snacks.   3. Eat smaller meals and snacks throughout the day.   4. Don't eat when you aren't hungry, and don't overeat when you are.   5. Relax while you eat.   6. Eat local foods that are in season at the time.   7. Eat organic foods.   8. Eat lots of fruits and vegetables. 9. Eat high-quality proteins.   10. Eat foods that are high in fiber.   11. Drink lots of water every day.   12. Eat a natural foods diet that works best for you.

III   1. T   2. T   3. F   4. T   5. F   6. T   7. T   8. F   9. T   10. T   11. F   12. F

IV-A

nouns	verbs	adjectives
sanctuary	tackle	ultimate
	implement	local
	facilitates	abundant
		organic
		regular
		chock-full
		unique

IV-B   1. organic   2. sanctuary   3. implement   4. local   5. tackle 6. abundant   7. regular   8. facilitates   9. ultimate   10. unique   11. chock-full

IV-C   Enzymes are to the body what spark plugs are to the engine of a car. Meaning, enzymes are like the spark plugs of the human body.

V-B   1. I won't be able to go shopping today.   2. We'll bring snacks to feed the children.   3. You'll have more energy if you eat more consistently throughout the day.   4. We'll eat a family meal once a day.   5. She'll only buy produce that has been grown locally.   6. He'll eat organic food whenever it's possible.   7. You'll increase your fiber intake by eating black beans.   8. She'll try to drink more water.

VI   1. High-fiber, fresh, natural organic fruits, vegetables, and legumes; whole grains; and high-quality organically and sustainably produced meats, dairy, and seafood.   2. We need to hydrate our cells so they function properly, and water brings in nutrients and removes wastes, promoting routes to digestive wellness.

Happiness boosters

I-B   1. i   2. c   3. f   4. g   5. e   6. b   7. j   8. a   9. h   10. d

III   1. F   2. T   3. F   4. T   5. T   6. F   7. F

IV-A   1. a   2. b   3. a   4. b   5. c   6. b   7. a   8. a   9. b   10. b

IV-B If instead of doing nothing when we come home from work we turn to our hobbies or other activities that challenge us, that we enjoy and that we care about, we are more likely to get a second wind and replenish our emotional bank.

V-B 1. too, 2. very 3. too 4. too 5. too 6. too 7. very

VI If you are active and involved in productive and meaningful activities, you will be happier both in your personal and professional life.

Mental gremlins

I-B 1. d 2. f 3. h 4. i 5. a 6. e 7. c 8. g 9. j 10. b

I-C Fear, anger, anxiety, self-consciousness, perfectionism, stubbornness, lack of motivation

III 1. b 2. g 3. e 4. f 5. a 6. c 7. d

IV-B 1. self-conscious 2. self-destructive 3. self-defeating 4. self-image 5. self-esteem 6. self-condemning 7. self-critical

V-B 1. Fear actually can paralyze you. 2. Self-critical, negative perfectionists can never do enough. 3. Some athletes simply lack the drive to become the best they can be. 4. You can't perform well if you're afraid of embarrassing yourself. You can't buy motivation; you can't obtain it from someone else. 5. This is unfortunate because in sports you must learn how to fail successfully./"Others can help motivate you, but basically it must come from you, and it must be a constant desire to do your very best at all times and under any circumstances."

VI To succeed, you must have a positive self-concept and overcome the seven self-defeating thoughts and behaviors, known as gremlins, that undermine performance.

Symptoms of depression

I-B 1. d 2. a 3. h 4. l 5. b 6. k 7. e 8. c 9. g 10. i 11. f 12. j

I-C The main idea of this excerpt is to help parents find out how vulnerable their teenage children may be to depression.

III 1. a 2. b 3. a 4. a 5. b

IV-A 1a. shift 1b. shifted 2a. access 2b. access 3a. alert 3b. alert 4a. steer 4b. Steer 5a. stress 5b. stressed 6a. switch 6b. switched

IV-B Have you communicated to your son that he's now the man of the house?

V-B 1. She has taught for a long time. 2. You went to the movies. 3. They were sick. 4. We learned English. 5. Has he gone to the movies? 6. Have you taught for a long time? 7. Were they sick? 8. Have they learned English?

VI 1. Loss of an important family member or friend 2. Parents' marital problems 3. Switching of schools

9. CHILDREN AND PARENTS

Positive parenting

I-B 1. e 2. d 3. a 4. b 5. c

I-C Both the parents and the children will benefit from positive parenting.

III 1. a 2. b 3. a 4. a 5. b 6. b

IV-A 1. function 2. encounter 3. destination 4. significant 5. influence
6. proverb

V 1. **Homonyms:** *positive*: definition 1; *return*: definition 2; *brief*: definition 2;
kid: definition 1; *function*: definition 3. 2. **Homophones:** principle, whether,
whole, taught, praise

VI Examples: 1. Including the unspoken as well as the spoken word is
important since it is the most powerful force in shaping a child's life. 2. Parents
who praise each of their children at least twice a day maintain a positive
relationship regardless of the problems they encounter.

The power of early experience

I-B 1. d 2. f 3. a 4. i 5. b 6. h 7. e 8. g 9. c

I-C Your child won't eat healthy food; you feed him the nutrient-poor
substitutes; he becomes accustomed to these foods; he won't eat the healthy food
you offer. By the time your child outgrows these dietary limitations, his food
habits are set in place and harder to change.

III 1. Early in life 2. Kids are naturally wired to follow daily routines and
rituals. 3. Eat breakfast every day. 4. Fruit and vegetables 5. Special
occasions like birthdays, vacations, or holidays 6. Lunch and dinner 7. Rarely,
perhaps reserved for parties or dining out 8. Water should be served at every
meal.

IV-A 1. verb 2. noun 3. noun 4. adjective 5. verb 6. noun 7. adjective
8. verb

IV-B 1. adopt 2. dietary 3. shape 4. preferences 5. routines 6. battle
7. cycle 8. Nutritional

IV-C Fruit or vegetables are the go-to snack if you are hungry before a meal.

V-B **Count:** child diet, battle, parents, wall, problem, cycle, food, substitutes,
limitations, habits, place, researchers, children, ways, routines, rituals, day,
patterns, ideas, fruits, vegetables, grains, protein, snack, desserts, ice-cream
sundaes, cake, pie, experiences, occasions, birthdays, vacations, holidays, lunch,
dinner, breakfast, syrups, sauces, doses, parties, beverage, examples, habits,
theories, family, kids, leader

Noncount: nature, power, future, life, dairy, butter, ketchup, sugar, soda pop, water

VI 1. It is important to establish healthy food routines when children are young
so they will get into the habit of healthy eating throughout their lives.
2. Eat breakfast every day; eat fruit or vegetables as snacks if you are hungry
before meals; sugary desserts should be saved for holidays.

Household chores

I-B 1. d 2. c 3. g 4. f 5. e 6. b 7. h 8. a

I-C "What can we do so that our kids complete these chores without our
nagging?"

III Checked items: 1, 3, 4, 5, 6, 7, 8, 11

IV-A 1. prioritize 2. discard 3. prevent 4. involve 5. delegate
6. distributed 7. neglect 8. reserve

V-B   Talk about why the tasks have to be done.; Have a family meeting about what needs to be done.; Sit down as a family, and list the household responsibilities.; Figure out who does what, when, and for how long.; Agree on a way to remind everyone of chores.; Discuss what the family should do if anyone, including parents, neglects to fulfill a responsibility.

VI   Children will appreciate their role in family life if they believe their views are being heard. When this occurs, they are more likely to be cooperative and responsible, and the parents will have helped to develop their children's self-discipline.

Establishing yourself as coach

I-B   1. f   2. i   3. a   4. j   5. c   6. h   7. d   8. k   9. e   10. g   11. b

I-C   Instilling good habits in the team's players; Helping players learn good habits through respecting the coach and the coach's position; Teaching players to listen to the coach and to respond to the coach's signal; Setting a good example through the coach's discipline; The coach must be aware of the players' distractions.; Coaches must learn how long their players can pay attention without getting bored or restless.

III   1. f,   2. a,   3. e,   4. c,   5. b,   6. d

IV-A

nouns	verbs	adjectives
habits	assess	inflated
authority	set	valuable
position	attend to	
	respect	
	refocus	
	position	

IV-B   1. position   2. habits   3. valuable   4. respect   5. inflated   6. attend to   7. authority   8. set   9. assess   10. refocus

V-B   1. to   2. for   3. of   4. about   5. in   6. of   7. in   8. about

VI   1. The coach is responsible for setting a good example.   2. Keeping children active is the best way to keep them from getting bored or restless.

10. FREE TIME, FUN TIME

Visiting thrift stores

I-B   1. b   2. c   3. g   4. a   5. d   6. e   7. h   8. f

I-C   Time

III   1. T   2. F   3. F   4. T   5. F   6. T   7. T   8. F

IV-A   1. f   2. g   3. c   4. d   5. a   6. e   7. b

IV-B   Thrift stores are usually connected to a charity and take in donated items in any ol' condition. If you are lucky, things are organized by color and garment type, but a boutique it ain't.

IV-C   1. c   2. b   3. a   4. i   5. h   6. d   7. e   8. f   9. g

V-B   1. I'm going shopping for shoes, but I'm not going to spend more than one hundred dollars.   2. I studied algebra for five hours, but I failed the test.   3. The manager rejected my plans, so I've got to change them.   4. He hung the clothes out to dry hours ago, but they are still wet.   5. We can broil fish on the grill tonight, or we can cook it in the oven.   6. The members complained loudly about the heat, but they remained to give their opinions about the project.

VI   Used, inexpensive clothing that can be interesting, unique, and creative

Spirituality and meditation

I-B   1. b   2. c   3. d   4. h   5. f   6. e   7. a   8. g

I-C   homeostasis, equilibrium, symmetry

III   1. F   2. T   3. T   4. F   5. T   6. T   7. F   8. F   9. T   10. T

IV-A   1. f   2. e   3. d   4. c   5. b   6. a

IV-B   1. symmetry   2. behavior   3. Turning inward   4. efficiently   5. retreat
6. Fortunately

VI   1. She luckily remembered to take her keys.   2. We surely will be on time for the movie.   3. I clearly need to change some of my behaviors.   4. He strangely doesn't like to relax on the weekends.   5. They honestly don't like going to the mountains.   6. I personally wouldn't recommend jogging at night.   7. She surprisingly knows how to play several different instruments.   8. We obviously can't take a broken car on the trip.

VII   1. Spirituality provides all of us techniques to slow down, turn inward, reduce the negative physiological effects of chronic stress on our brain and body, and help us to generate a more pleasing sense of balance and homeostasis. Engaging in spirituality is a great way to stop, reflect, meditate, and relax to take a respite from our hurried lifestyle.   2. Meditation can help you to slow down and turn inward for balance and symmetry. Your brain can adapt to a chaotic world, but it will function more efficiently over a longer period of time if you provide moments of inward reflection and rest. Meditation offers one technique to achieve such inner peace.

Success at surfing

I-B   1. f   2. j   3. m   4. k   5. a   6. i   7. b   8. l   9. c   10. d   11. e   12. g
13. h

I-C   Surfing is considered a "personal activity" because it is a sport that involves just you, your board, and a wave.

III   1. T   2. T   3. F   4. T   5. F   6. T   7. F   8. F   9. F   10. T   11. F
12. F   13. T

IV-A   1. h   2. i   3. d   4. e   5. f   6. b   7. c   8. a   9. g

IV-B   1. shooting baskets   2. obligation   3. garden-variety   4. timeless
5. melt away   6. come of age   7. giving yourself wholly   8. fluid
9. cost-benefit analysis

V-B   Pipeline, Oahu; 1. C   2. P   3. C   4. P   5. P   6. C   7. P

VI   Success is completely defined by the participant.

Backpacking into the wilderness

I-B 1. m 2. n 3. h 4. k 5. d 6. e 7. i 8. b 9. c 10. l 11. g 12. j
13. f 14. a

I-C Stars, wilderness, water, earth, world, nature, summit, lake, crag, vista,
mountains, deserts, forests, meadows, landscape, natural world, land

III 1. b 2. c 3. a 4. c 5. b 6. b

IV-A 1. a 2. b 3. a 4. c 5. a 6. b 7. c 8. a

IV-B By experiencing the wilderness directly, by being in touch with the land, we
can learn how valuable—how essential—it is, and that we must try to preserve
and restore our still-beautiful world.

V-C 1. pregame 2. indiscreet 3. infertile 4. prearrange 5. renew 6. preheat
7. inappropriate 8. repaint 9. inactive 10. reassemble 11. preceded

VI You gain that indefinable feeling of rightness, of being with instead of against
the earth, that gives the deepest contentment. You explore yourself and experience
nature. By walking through a landscape, you enter into it and begin to grasp that
you are a part of the earth.